PATTI GALLAGHER MANSFIELD

Everyday HOLINESS
Bringing the Holy Spirit Home

Amor
DEUS
PUBLISHING

Everyday Holiness
Bringing the Holy Spirit Home
Patti Gallagher Mansfield

Cover image: Shutterstock.com
Cover and book design: Amor Deus Publishing Design Department

For information regarding permission, write to:
Amor Deus Publishing
Attention: Permissions Dept.
4727 North 12th Street
Phoenix, AZ 85014

ISBN 978–1–61956–249–3

Third Edition August 2014
10 9 8 7 6 5 4 3

Original edition entitled *More of God: Inspirational Selections from the Notebook Column*, published by Franciscan University Press, Stubenville, Ohio © 1991.

Revised edition published in 2002 by Noah's Ark Creations Pte Ltd, 29 Ettrick Terrace, Singapore 458592
Tel: (65) 62421167 Fax: (65) 64457387 Email: noahs.ark@postl.com

Published and printed in the United States of America by Amor Deus Publishing an imprint of Vesuvius Press Incorporated.

♻ Text printed on 30% post–consumer waste recycled paper.

For additional inspirational books visit us at AmorDeus.com

Dedication

I lovingly dedicate this collection of columns to the three men who have encouraged me to publish them:

Mr. Peter Gallagher, my father, who has given me the gift of life and whose love has reflected so well the love of my Father in heaven.

Fr. Andrew Becnel, OSB, my spiritual father, who taught me the importance of *douceur, abandon, humilité, confiance.*

Fr. George Kosicki, CSB, my spiritual mentor and friend, who was an icon of the Father of mercies in my life.

Endorsements

Johnnette S. Benkovic
Founder, Women of Grace®
Host, EWTN Television and Radio

Wisdom is a supernatural gift of the Holy Spirit that helps us see the hand of God moving in and through all things. And in *Everyday Holiness* it is wisdom that Patti Gallagher Mansfield gives us. From the mundane to the extraordinary Patti proves that every moment shimmers with grace. Through charming storytelling, gentle instruction, and profound insight she shares events from her life that convince us God is always with us and He is always about a work in us. An encouraging retrospective that edifies and enlightens and leads us to beg God for the eyes to see.

Sr. Briege McKenna, OSC
Author, *Miracles Do Happen*

As a wife and mother, Patti is a witness to truly Catholic family values both in her writing and speaking. I pray that this book will touch the lives of very many people.

Babsie Bleasdell
Word of Life, Founder. Trinidad

Patti was among the first to be baptized in the Holy Spirit in the response to Pope Saint John XXIII's prayer for a New Pentecost. She is a gift to the whole Church as sister, friend, wife, mother and daughter. Her columns help us all to find sanctity in the everyday things of ordinary life.

Marilyn Quirk
Foundress, Magnificat Ministry to Catholic Women

Patti has been to me and to many, a sister, a friend and a model of Our Lady. Her life has mirrored Mary's total yes in her everyday life as she has walked in the Spirit. "I am the servant of the Lord , let it be done unto me according to your word."

Fr. Harold Cohen, SJ
Closer Walk Ministries

Patti has been an inspiration to me by the witness of her life and by her proclamation of the Word of life. May this book open many, many others to the Spirit within her, the Spirit who gives witness to Jesus, the Spirit who glorifies Jesus (John 15:26, 16:14).

Fr. Michael Scanlan, TOR
Chancellor Emeritus
Franciscan University of Steubenville

Patti Gallagher Mansfield is a special gift to all of us who have witnessed the renewal in the Catholic Church by the power of the Holy Spirit since Vatican II. Patti represented a fervent Catholic who never needed to compromise either a full Catholic life and devotion on the one hand or the fresh new work of the Holy Spirit on the other.

She was there, not just as an inspiring speaker and leader but before all else, as a wife and mother. She, Al, and the family were first of all a family together and she spoke and wrote from within that family context. Her columns have touched the hearts and enlightened the minds of vast numbers who count on her integrated Catholic Charismatic Renewal and family perspective.

Al and Patti Mansfield with their four children, daughters-in-law and six of their seven grandchildren. The grandchildren are wearing their baptismal stoles made by Grandma!

Foreword

For several years, every time I met someone from the United States at one of the international meetings of the Charismatic Renewal, I hastened to ask if he or she knew Patti Gallagher. My question usually caused a slight embarrassment. It would seem that, in America, the name Gallagher can have several different pronunciations. My way of pronouncing it was not among these. But even after I learned to pronounce it correctly, no one seemed to have heard of a person by that name. Then, just as I was about to give up the search, someone suddenly showed a sign of recognition: "But of course, you mean Patti Mansfield!"

And so I learned all at once that Patti was no longer called Gallagher but Mansfield, that she was happily married, the mother at that time of two children and known on a national level in the Charismatic Renewal.

But I must explain when and how her name had impressed me. I was on a plane going to the United States together with a small group of other Italians to take part in the big ecumenical and charismatic meeting in Kansas City in July 1977. Someone gave me a copy of *New Covenant* magazine to read. Among the articles there was one written by one of the participants of the first Catholic Charismatic retreat who, at that time, was called Patti Gallagher. At a certain point Patti wrote: "As I witnessed the rapid movement of God's Spirit all over the world, I heard Jesus' words addressed to me: 'Blessed are the eyes that see what you see.'"

I was deeply impressed by these words and they kept coming back into my mind during the whole journey, thus helping me to overcome the diffidence that I still felt towards the charismatic phenomenon. It was clear that her words were not simply a quotation from the Bible. It was rather a testimony showing that what is related in the Gospels was again happening in the world, that those words of Jesus were once again being fulfilled.

So when Patti Mansfield's *Notebook* columns started to appear in *New Covenant*, I never missed one of them. When I finally decided to write to her to settle my debt of gratitude, I knew through her columns nearly everything about her family and I was able to ask her about her children.

However, it is not a question of simple scenes of family life. There is a common line of thought going through Patti Mansfield's *Notebook* columns which I would sum up in this way: "the Charismatic Renewal in everyday life." Through these simple testimonies made by the mother of a family, a woman and a lay Christian actively involved in the service of the Kingdom, one thing appears clear. It is clear that the Holy Spirit is not only committed to renewing the great activities of the Church—theology, evangelization, liturgy, prayer—but even reaches the very heart of Christian life, making of the whole of life, with nothing excluded, "a living sacrifice, holy and acceptable to God," as St. Paul exhorts in Romans 12:2.

Thank you then to our sister Patti Gallagher Mansfield, who, once again with this collection of her *Notebook* columns, reminds us of the words of Jesus: "Blessed are the eyes that see what you see."

Fr. Raniero Cantalamessa, OFM Cap.
Preacher to the Papal Household

Contents

Al and Patti Mansfield with their seven grandchildren in
Covington, Louisiana, 2013.
Caroline, Molly, Claire, Catherine, John,
Will, and Michael

 Introduction

Tucked inside my Bible is a little card with the following prayer by St. Thérèse of Lisieux which I love.

Grant me Your grace, most merciful Jesus that it may be with me and continue with me to the end. Grant me always to will and to desire that which is most acceptable to You and which pleases You best. Let Your will be mine and let my will always follow Yours and agree perfectly with it. Amen.

One day at a conference we were asked to write down our deepest desires. On the other side of this prayer card, I wrote the following: "I desire to be holy, to be a saint. I desire to be greatly used by God to draw huge numbers of people to know and love Jesus Christ. I desire to live a life consecrated to Mary as a true daughter of the Church. I desire to be a loving wife and mother to the glory of God. Amen."

Now you might stop reading right here and conclude that I'm obviously suffering from delusions of grandeur. But as those who live close to me will readily attest, I am an ordinary woman, living in the midst of everyday circumstances and concerns. My boundless desires stem directly from the fact that I have been caught up in an extraordinary outpouring of God's Holy Spirit. "The love of God has been poured into our hearts through the Holy Spirit who has been given to us" (Romans 5:5). I can now hope for the very things that once seemed impossible, because I've learned that "with God *all things* are possible."

Like my patroness, St. Thérèse, the Little Flower, I've come to believe from personal experience that I can never hope for too much from the good God. In her words, "I know now that all my expectations shall be fulfilled—Yes, the Lord will perform marvels for me which will infinitely surpass my immense desires!" This happens, not because I am worthy—far from it—but rather because I am small and unworthy, yet full of trust in His merciful love. An antiphon in the Divine Office reads, "Surrender to God and He will do everything for you." Even a modern day Teresa, Blessed Mother Teresa of Calcutta, tells us that holiness is *not* the luxury of a few, but the vocation of every Christian. We're *all* called to be saints.

Believe me when I say that as a youngster I had no special plans to give myself to God. Sure, I wanted to be good and pleasing to others, but beyond that, my relationship with Jesus was primarily one of convenience—my own. I prayed very earnestly whenever I wanted something from the Lord, usually describing exactly *what* should happen, *how* it should happen and *when* it should happen—just in case He couldn't figure it out Himself! I never even seriously considered a vocation to religious life. In fact, I had my future all mapped out according to a carefully devised plan for happiness.

So I was, you might say, surprised by grace when, at the age of 20, on what's now called "The Duquesne Weekend," the Lord revealed Himself to me, baptized me in the Holy Spirit and placed a call on my life. One encounter with the Lord in the chapel of the Ark and the Dove Retreat House in Pittsburgh, Pennsylvania taught me more about God than I could have acquired through a lifetime of study. The words of St. Augustine capture so well what I experienced when I was baptized in the Holy Spirit: "You have made us for Yourself, O Lord, and our hearts are restless until they rest in You." The psalmist David writes, "Taste and see that the Lord is good." Yes, He is good. I have tasted and I know the goodness of the living God.

All that I have written about in this collection of columns flows from my experience on the Duquesne Weekend. Time and again I make mention of this grace of the Baptism in the Holy Spirit because I believe it is available for every Christian who will ask Jesus for it in faith. If you want more of God, if you want to experience His action in your everyday life, then seek the Baptism in the Holy Spirit. These columns reflect a spirituality that is Catholic, Charismatic and Marian.

The standard joke in the Mansfield family is this: "Watch out or Mom will write a column about you!" And it's true. Since it is in the midst of my life as a wife and mother that the Holy Spirit teaches me, my columns are filled with personal examples. Pope Paul VI in his address to women at the close of Vatican II said that women know how to make the truth "sweet, tender and accessible." That has been my goal in these columns: to make the truth sweet, tender and accessible. I thank my husband Al and my children, Mark, Peter, Marie-Thérèse and Patrick for permitting me to share our family life with all of you.

I pray that the Holy Spirit will breathe over these pages and over the lives of those who read it.

Now to Him who by the power at work within us is able to do far more abundantly than all that we can ask or think, to Him be glory in the church and in Christ Jesus to all generations, forever and ever. Amen.
(Ephesians 3:20-21).

Patti Gallagher Mansfield
October 1, 1990
Feast of St. Thérèse of Lisieux

Introduction
to the Second Edition

Pope Saint John Paul II has presented us with a magnificent vision of the new millennium in his Apostolic Letter, *Novo Millennio Ineunte.* The first time I read this letter, I was very reassured because his words corresponded to my deeply held conviction: Everyone is called to be a saint! No exceptions! That means you and me!

But how can we become saints? The Holy Father gives us the answer: Contemplate the face of Jesus and follow the inspirations of the Holy Spirit. This is what the Baptism in the Spirit is all about: focusing ourselves on the Lord Jesus Christ and surrendering ourselves completely to the action of the Holy Spirit. And that is what this book is all about too.

Marriage is the vocation to which my husband and I have been called by God. It is as husband and wife, father and mother, grandmother and grandfather that we are challenged to become saints. Family life is a school of holiness. Each day we are confronted with the need to die to ourselves and to live for God and for others. For us married people, the "others" are primarily those in our own homes.

These columns appeared over a eight year period in *New Covenant* magazine (1985–1992). I have removed the references to each month and offer them to the reader as simple vignettes about everyday holiness. When I wrote these reflections, I was in the midst of raising our four young children. Now Mark, Peter and Marie-Thérèse are attorneys and Patrick is an entrepreneur. Time has indeed passed and the little children whose stories are contained in these pages have become accomplished adults. What remains the same, however, is the presence of the Lord Jesus and His Holy Spirit in our everyday lives.

At this writing we have seven grandchildren who are our joy and delight! The eldest grandchild, Catherine, has already read these columns and discovered many family secrets!

May these simple stories from the Mansfield family inspire you to seek God—yes, more of God, in your own daily routine. Hold on to the ideal of *Everyday Holiness*. Strive with all your might to become what Pope Saint John Paul II called us to be—saints of the new millennium! Pope Francis is looking to us families to be agents in the New Evangelization. He wrote, "The family which experiences the joy of faith communicates it naturally.... It is a joy which we experience daily, amid the little things of life." May you and your families know that joy and share it with the world!

Patti Gallagher Mansfield
August 22, 2014
Feast of the Queenship of Mary

What Did I Ever Do?

"What did I ever do to deserve this?" I kept asking as I stood looking out over the muddy Monongahela River from my dormitory window. It was September, 1964, and I had just arrived at Duquesne University in Pittsburgh to begin my freshman year. The resident assistant told me how lucky I was to have a room "with a view." "Some view!", I grumbled inwardly. I was convinced I had made a huge mistake by coming to Duquesne. It certainly wasn't my first choice.

You see, I had set my heart on going to Boston College after a visit to its beautiful campus. Although I was accepted at Boston College, I received no financial aid. A full tuition scholarship from Duquesne lured me there instead. After my choice was made, I won a larger scholarship which could have been used at any school, including Boston College. However, I decided to hold fast to my choice of Duquesne, even though I had never seen the campus.

Words cannot describe my dismay when I first laid eyes on Duquesne University that September. It was thoroughly unimpressive compared to Boston College. Many departments were housed in old homes along the Bluff of the river. Other homes were boarded up and vacant. A few poor families still remained in the dying neighborhood. I found the surroundings absolutely depressing. Victory Gardens in the middle of the campus was made to look like a park in the Duquesne catalog; in actuality it was a small patch of grass. "I could be at beautiful Boston College or at any school in the country," I groaned, "and instead I chose this awful place."

That first night on campus my parents took me out to dinner. My disappointment with Duquesne was so intense I broke down crying. Weakened by my tears, my father was too upset to even finish his meal. "Drive home with us, Honey," Daddy said. "You can transfer to Boston College next semester."

"No," I protested, playing the martyr, "I'll stick it out here for a semester." So, reluctantly, they left me in Pittsburgh.

Within just a few weeks, as I got to know the students and faculty at Duquesne, I really grew to love the school and decided to make it my home. That decision profoundly affected the course of my entire life. Although I didn't realize it at the time, it was God's providence that led me to Duquesne. He had plans for me there I would never have dreamed nor imagined possible.

In God's inscrutable wisdom, He chose to visit Duquesne University in February, 1967, when a group of us made a weekend retreat on the theme of the Holy Spirit. Until that time, my prayer followed these general lines: "Lord, bless my plans, do my will, according to my timetable. Amen."

During that retreat I realized my deep need for conversion. On Saturday night I knelt in the chapel and made an unconditional surrender to God. I prayed that I might do the Father's will, learn to follow Jesus and be filled with His love. In answer to my simple prayer of faith, God baptized me in His Holy Spirit. As I fell prostrate before the Blessed Sacrament I felt inundated with the incredibly merciful, totally unmerited love of God. Within a short time I was joined by some of the other students in the chapel where we experienced a sovereign outpouring of the Spirit of the living God. From that moment on, my life has never been the same.

That retreat, now known as the "Duquesne Weekend," was much more than a moving personal experience. It marked the beginning of the worldwide outpouring of God's Spirit we call the Catholic Charismatic Renewal. The spark that was ignited at Duquesne has become a fire that is inflaming the hearts of millions of people across the face of the earth! God visited Duquesne. It was His choice. What a privilege to be there when He arrived!

Shortly after my conversion, I was walking along the Bluff, looking out over the muddy Monongahela River once again. It was the same view I had seen on my first day on campus, but I was a different person. Gratitude welled up within my heart for the grace of experiencing His visitation. "What did I ever do to deserve this, Jesus?" I asked in prayer, filled with amazement and awe. Of course, I had done nothing to deserve it. No one could ever merit God's gift of the Holy Spirit. But, in His mercy, the Lord guided me to a place where I could encounter His love. Choosing Duquesne was *not* a huge mistake after all. In fact, it was one of the greatest graces of my entire life!

In the summer of 1988 I returned to Duquesne for the first time since my graduation in 1968—a kind of 20 year reunion. A sense of awe came over me as I considered how the Holy Spirit has moved since the Duquesne Weekend. Walking across the small campus, I marveled anew at what a humble place Duquesne really is.

God didn't choose the most impressive, prestigious or influential school for His first stop in this modern day outpouring of the Holy Spirit. Instead, He visited an ordinary group of people at an ordinary campus in the Pittsburgh hills. God's wisdom and His way always defy human understanding. Perhaps the Duquesne story serves as a reminder that we can never merit His gifts. Rather, it is the Father's good pleasure to give us the Kingdom. Of ourselves we deserve nothing, in Jesus we receive *everything!* Praise God for His grace and mercy!

 Funny Paper Time

Comic strips or "funny papers" or "funnies", as we call them, are important to us as a family. My favorite cartoon is pinned up on the refrigerator right now. It's a farm scene of a papa bull standing next to his little son. They're gazing off into the distance at the famous cow jumping over the moon. The caption reads, "Son, your mother is a remarkable woman!"

I still laugh every time I see it. But the funnies mean more to our family than just a good chance to laugh. They have forged a bond among us.

The interest in the funny papers was started by my husband. As a little boy he loved it when his dad read the funnies to him. So starting with our first child, each little Mansfield has been introduced to the Sunday ritual of reading the funnies with Dad. Sometime after dinner Al announces, "Funny Paper Time!" and the couch becomes a gathering place for the children with their daddy. We have photos in our album of Al with one, then two, then three little ones next to him.

One Sunday a few years ago when my husband was away, I tried to replace him as reader. Though I thought I was reading the funnies just the way he does (each comic strip has a special intonation), the children weren't satisfied. They wanted to wait until Dad got home to read to them. It just wasn't the same without him! Now when he's gone on Sunday we save the papers until a weekday when he's home. We transfer Funny Paper Time as though it were a "moveable feast."

Of course the children have grown and time has passed since this tradition first began. When our oldest child began to read for himself he was often missing from the couch at Funny Paper Time. That's understandable. When our second child began to read, it seemed as though he would outgrow this Sunday tradition as well. One Sunday he told us that since he could read the funnies by himself, he'd rather go out to play ball than sit with Dad. But no sooner had he left, when he returned.

"Gee, Mom," Peter said, "I think I'll stay and let Dad read me the funnies after all, because I may not always have this time with him."

I may not always have this time with him. What an amazing truth this young child had grasped! There was something precious to be shared by simply being with his father right then, and he didn't want to miss it. As he climbed on the couch and nestled under his dad's arm to listen to the funnies, my little boy taught me a valuable lesson worth recalling.

Time is passing. We won't have this year, this day, this moment to live over again. How much we need to cherish not only the present moment, but also those people who are with us in the present moment, for we shall not always have them. Circumstances or death may take them away.

It was my dear father-in-law, Alton W. Mansfield, who started the funny paper tradition. In 1985 he was called home to the Lord. During one of our last visits to his bedside, I noticed the funny papers open beside him—a touching reminder of special moments he shared with my husband so long ago.

Funny Paper Time was and still is a simple way for us to be together as a family. Let's cherish those moments in our families and communities. Even in simple things may we learn to be present to those we love. We shall not have this time again.

P.S. Thirty years later my husband now reads the funnies to his grandchildren and Catherine, Peter's eldest child, is the one who loves them the most!

Stuck in the Mud

"You deserve a break today," rings the familiar slogan beckoning us to buy hamburgers rather than cook dinner. At times we all feel like we really do deserve a break. For me such a time came after serving at one of our first regional Catholic Charismatic conferences.

After many months of preparation and the joy of the conference itself, fatigue set in. I had not yet learned that after having done all that is required we should say, "We are unworthy servants; we have only done what was our duty" (Luke 17:10). Instead I felt that after all our hard work, we definitely deserved a break.

Some friends offered us their cabin in the woods for a family vacation right after the conference. Eagerly we packed ourselves, our children, the food, playpen, high chair and toys into the car. Off we headed for a glorious, restful, quiet week in the country. Or so we thought.

Once we arrived at the cabin, everything seemed to go wrong. The baby didn't sleep well. Our other child came down with a cold. It rained day after day; then came the hail and threats of flooding.

But the final blow was when one of the boys climbed onto a shelf (in the early morning hours) and all the games and books came thundering down on top of him.

"That's it!", said my husband. "We're going home!" The children weren't happy and neither were we. What was planned as a relaxing time together had turned into a tense and frustrating fiasco. So we cleaned up, packed all our paraphernalia into the car to return home.

But the ground was so soggy that when my husband tried to back the car out, we got stuck in the mud. Nothing we tried seemed to help; the car wouldn't budge. Since there was no phone in the cabin, my husband flagged someone down who called a tow truck for us from the nearest town.

What a sight we must have been! All our belongings had been unpacked to lighten the car; the baby was getting fussy, and swarms of mosquitoes were eating us up.

We were feeling pretty sorry for ourselves when our three-year-old son, Mark, asked for his toy guitar and began to strum. To our amazement God spoke to us through the song of this little child. He sang from Romans 8:

> *If God is for us, who can be against,*
> *If the Spirit of God has set us free?*
> *I know that nothing in this world*
> *can ever take us from His love.*

As he warbled out verse after verse of Romans 8 we began to see our circumstances in a new way. The Lord was right there with us, wanting to communicate His love and joy even in this frustrating experience. And just in case the message of Romans 8 wasn't clear enough, guess what he sang as an encore?

> *And the Father will dance as on a day of joy,*
> *He will rejoice over you and renew you by His love.*

We seemed to be a pretty sorry crew for the Father to be dancing over, yet our little troubadour continued singing:

"Shout for joy all you His people,
for Yahweh your God is in your midst!"

As we returned home I was surprised how refreshed I felt. My heart was full of joy and gratitude at having been touched by God. Although I didn't get the "break" I thought I deserved, the Lord gave me something I needed even more. He came to meet me when I was stuck in the mud with the reminder that He is present in all circumstances. And nothing can ever separate me from His love!

 # The Tooth Fairy

"Mom?", a little voice called to me, "I'm afraid my tooth will get lost if I put it under my pillow. I wrapped it up in a pink tissue, and it's on my nightstand right now."

I assured my daughter that I would tell the tooth fairy just where to find it. This was actually the second little pearl she had lost. The first tooth fell out while she was sleeping, and we never found it. To her joy, she could hold this newly lost little tooth in her palm, show it off to the family, and even brush it to get "all the yucky stuff off." Somehow I hadn't been able to convince her that getting the "yucky stuff" off the teeth still in her mouth was more important than polishing up the one she had just lost.

We've joked a lot about the tooth fairy. My little girl knows that Mom is the one who visits the bedrooms by night to deposit a quarter in exchange for a pearly white. Since I'm expecting a new baby I had told her before bedtime that the tooth fairy might walk instead of fly this time because of her added weight.

When my daughter was finally asleep, I made my visit. I kissed and blessed her, collecting the pink tissue with its precious contents and leaving behind 25 cents on my way out of her room. It was not my first nocturnal visit, and it won't be my last!

Assuming the role of tooth fairy again has flooded my mind with memories of years past. For instance, there was the day I was feeding my first child, Mark, and the metal spoon hit something hard in his mouth. You can't imagine my excitement when I saw a tiny speck of white peeking out when my baby smiled. It was as if no other child had ever cut a tooth before! My husband jokingly told me to be sure to have this seven-month-old baby brush his new tooth every day.

Then I recalled how shocked our son, Mark, was when he found out that children lose their baby teeth. After reflection our little one announced with great generosity that when his teeth fell out he wanted to send them to "the poor children who didn't have any."

Since we had been giving away extra clothes and toys, he thought his idea was perfectly logical. Of course, when Mark was older this same young man tried convincing the tooth fairy that 25 cents was too little to leave for teeth these days, considering the impact of inflation!

Then came memories of chipped teeth, blackened teeth, extracted teeth, teeth that still need to be straightened, and teeth that didn't get brushed. "Oh, you mean I have to do this every day for the rest of my life, Mom?" Just think, at this moment the child within me has teeth buds already formed under the surface of the gums. Before long I'll be in search of a new little tooth in the mouth of a new little baby. Yes, my days as a tooth fairy are not over yet!

To someone who hasn't shared such experiences, all this tooth business may seem insignificant. Why make such a fuss over a few teeth? But to a mother, these are memories to cherish and joys to anticipate. Playing tooth fairy is part of a mother's delight. Unfortunately, many women today will never experience such joy for themselves.

A few years ago I overheard the conversation of two young women. One was married; the other was engaged. Both agreed that they didn't ever want to have children. They reasoned that a family would interfere too much with their lives and their careers. As their conversation proceeded, it was clear that they felt that children were a nuisance and cost too much to raise. Why complicate a husband/wife relationship by the addition of children?

The more they conversed, the sadder I became. I grieved that these two women and so many like them have accepted such a negative, worldly attitude toward family life. Perhaps as they mature they will see things differently. No one will deny that one can find fulfillment in a career. However, there is a satisfaction that comes from caring for a family that cannot be measured in terms of a paycheck or prestige. Children aren't an interference, but rather an incarnation of the love of a husband and wife.

Scripture tells us that "Children are a blessing from the Lord, the fruit of the womb a reward" (Psalm 127:3). Of course, there are sacrifices and difficulties in raising a family. It's not easy to continually serve the needs of others, but the teaching of Scripture is absolutely true. Children are *indeed* a blessing from the Lord!

More than ever before we "tooth fairies" need to stand together and proclaim our love and respect for human life. Let's give clear witness to a world that has forgotten about the sacredness and beauty of new life. God's blessing and joy is ours because we have chosen to bear children.

Thirty years later our grandson John is about to lose a tooth any day. I understand that the tooth fairy now needs to pay at least a dollar for a pearly white!

Feed My Lambs

In July, 1987, I attended the New Orleans Congress on the Holy Spirit and World Evangelization. There were thousands of Catholic charismatics present from around the country. Again and again I met people who asked "What did you have, a boy or a girl? We've been praying for you."

I realized that through my columns in *New Covenant* magazine many people knew I was expecting a baby, but they never received a birth announcement. It's wonderful to know that I now have brothers and sisters all over the world who are interested in our latest addition.

Patrick John Mansfield arrived October 1, 1986. Eight pounds, 14 ounces of beautiful baby boy. By now he's a chubby, blue-eyed toddler. His precious Irish grin reveals four little teeth, and he makes mischief at every turn. Patrick's biggest problem is that at least two of us are kissing him all the time. The other children want to know how I ever managed being mother to a baby before they were old enough to help! With all the affection and attention lavished on Patrick, he will either grow up totally convinced of God's love or be spoiled beyond repair. Let's pray it is the former!

Each December I take a traditional Christmas picture of our children in front of the tree with their gifts. But last Christmas when Patrick was an infant, I decided to do something different. A few pieces of blue material, draped and corded, quickly transformed Marie-Thérèse into the Blessed Mother. With a sheet to cover his head and his bathrobe on, Mark Joseph played the part of his patron, St. Joseph. And after I found a tunic and head-piece for Peter, I handed him a toy lamb. "You be the shepherd, Peter." Of course, Baby Jesus was none other than our new little boy, Prince Patrick.

"Ok, everybody," I said, camera poised and ready to shoot, "Smile!" Then I changed my mind. "No, don't smile. Look holy. Marie-Thérèse, cross your hands over your chest. Mark, get serious and look at the baby. Peter, hold up that lamb where I can see it. Now we're ready. Hold it."

Before I could get my carefully posed nativity scene on film, the children dissolved into laughter. Their explanation? "Mom, we can't help it. Patrick smells like rotten eggs."

It was true. Baby Jesus was squirming and kicking, and as I got closer, he really did smell like rotten eggs. After a quick diaper change, the picture was taken and then the questions started.

"Mom, did Jesus ever cry? Did He coo like Patrick? Did He have toys? Did He like to be rocked? Did Jesus ever smell like rotten eggs?"

Yes, Jesus was "like us in all things but sin," Scripture tells us. It boggles our minds to consider it. Having Patrick in the family, especially at Christmastime, has made me more aware of what the Incarnation really means.

God truly became *one of us* when Jesus was born. He literally took on human flesh. Jesus was as dependent on Mary as Patrick is on me. Yes, He cried and cooed; He needed to be rocked and fed and changed.

My little Patrick has been a reminder of the tremendous humility of our God who came among us as a helpless child.

But more than that, Patrick has provided me with a new opportunity to love Jesus.

A good friend of mine, Marilyn Quirk, tells how she longed for an extended time of daily prayer after the birth of her fifth child. While her baby was napping, Marilyn tried to pray. But time and again the baby woke up. She just couldn't get the little one settled. Marilyn regretted ending her time of quiet prayer, so she lingered just a few moments more. Then the Lord spoke to her.

"Marilyn, do you love Me?"

"Yes, Lord," she replied. "You know that I love You."

What Jesus said to St. Peter long ago, He repeated to her,

"Feed my lamb."

Strengthened by His word, Marilyn got up quickly and with great joy, knowing that she would meet Jesus as she cared for her child, His little lamb.

You may not have a new baby, but there are surely other "lambs" in your life. It may be a moody teenager, a discouraged spouse, an elderly parent, or a lonely neighbor who needs to be refreshed and comforted and nourished through your love and attention.

Jesus Himself is waiting to meet you in them. He is Emmanuel—God with us. Whatever you do for one of His lambs, He counts it as done for Him. Rejoice!

Mama

"Mamamamamama!"

There he goes again. Just as I sat down to write this column I could hear my baby, Patrick, calling for me from another room. For the past hour he was playing with his dad and brothers. By now, he's tired. With that string of syllables he's telling me he needs my help to get ready for bed.

I've noticed that when each of my children started to speak they happily babbled their "Dadadada" sounds all day long. In times of play, exploration and excitement it was always "Dada," even though their Daddy was away at work. But when my little ones were tired, hungry, frightened or hurt they quickly changed their babble. With insistence and often with tears would they call out, "Mama, Mama!" Instinctively they knew that "Mama" was another word for "help." Simple as it is, the cry for help and the helping that follows is how bonding grows between mother and child.

Instead of being a distraction with his string of "Mamas" tonight, Patrick actually helped confirm what I wanted to write about today. It is significant that the Church calls us to celebrate the feast of Mary, the Mother of God on January 1. We are doing more than simply honoring her. Placed at the start of another year, this feast reminds us that in order to get through a new year of our Lord we need the help of the Mother of our Lord. Mary. Mother. Mama, as Patrick would call her.

There are probably many of you who can warm immediately to such thoughts. For you, Mary has been a "sign of sure hope and solace" throughout your lives. There is no conflict between loving Jesus and loving Mary. But I am sure there are many others who do not understand how Mary can have a place in your spiritual lives. Perhaps you have yet to experience Mary's love for you and the power of her intercession. In the Charismatic Renewal we refer to a moment, or moments of conversion and commitment to Jesus Christ. We speak of the experience of being baptized in the Holy Spirit. I believe there is also a "Marian Moment," a time of special grace, when we come to take Mary as our own, our mother. This "Marian Moment" is a gift, but it's a gift God longs to give to all of us if we are open.

It's often surprised me when Christians of other traditions discover Mary. Several years ago I was speaking at a retreat for Catholics and encouraging those present to seek a personal relationship with Mary. "Ask Jesus to introduce you to His mother," I said. Little did I know that one of the retreatants, Sally, was from a Four Square Gospel Church. The idea of relating to Mary was really foreign to her but she wanted to be open.

Later that evening Sally went into the chapel to pray. She knew Jesus and loved Him very much. "Introduce me to your mother, Jesus," she prayed. As Sally has described it, in the next moments, Mary came to her. As a loving mother, Mary took Sally into her arms and embraced her. From that moment on Sally knew she had a mother in heaven who loved her, who understood her struggles, who wanted to help her. As time passed Sally felt gradually drawn to join the Catholic Church.

A religious sister I know was working with the poor in New Orleans. She met a lovely Baptist woman in one of the housing projects who plied her with questions about Mary. She had seen the Pilgrim Statue of Our Lady of Fatima in someone's home and was intrigued.

"Do you think Mary might come to me?" the woman asked Sister.

"Surely, if you want her," Sister replied.

Imagine the surprise of her son, a Baptist minister, when he entered her home and saw the statue of Our Lady of Fatima.

"Don't say a word about her, Son!," protested the little lady. "I'm your mother. She's His mother. She stays!"

While remaining a Baptist, this simple woman literally welcomed Mary into her home and experienced the power of having a relationship with the mother of Jesus.

One last story. A nondenominational minister I know tells how he had reached an impasse in his prayer life. One day he locked himself in his office, determined not to leave until he had broken through in prayer to the Lord. As he prayed, the Holy Spirit began to lead him to passages in Scripture that spoke of Mary. He says he came under a spirit of conviction, because he had not shown enough respect for the mother of the Lord. He repented and determined never again to criticize or show dishonor for Mary, whom all generations should call blessed. As he did this, a breakthrough in prayer resulted. To those who are open, even brothers and sisters of other denominations, there can be a "Marian Moment"—a moment of grace in relation to Mary.

I'd like to close with the words of the *Memorare* of St. Bernard. *"Remember, O most gracious Virgin Mary, that never was it known that anyone who fled to your protection, implored your help or sought your intercession was left unaided."* Never was anyone left unaided! Quite a promise, don't you agree? If you haven't yet met Mary, your mother, your mama, and if you're in need of help right now, call on her. She loves you and she'll come to your aid.

A More Excellent Way

Years ago I read a little pamphlet by Archbishop Goodier, SJ, entitled *A More Excellent Way*. The author painted a picture of himself as a young novice, full of high hopes for his growth in the spiritual life. He studied and sought to understand and categorize the virtues. With a carefully constructed plan, he then set out to acquire them all. For the first week he'd work on humility. Week two he'd master patience, then well-guarded speech on week three. By the fourth week, he'd surely be ready to "put on love." In a month or so the young novice fully expected to "have an ecstasy and see the Lord!" As a much older and wiser man, this priest admitted he was still struggling for the virtue of his first week! Humility. Sound familiar?

There's no getting away from it. Humility is at the foundation of all growth in holiness. It could easily go on everyone's list of New Year's resolutions since pride is so entrenched in the human heart. Humility is pride's antidote. Scripture tells us, "God resists the proud but gives grace to the humble...Be humbled in the sight of the Lord and He will raise you high" (James 4:6, 10).

If we are humble before God, acknowledging who He is and who we are, then we can ask for what we will in utter confidence. Look at the Canaanite woman. Look at the centurion whose servant was ill. Knowing their unworthiness, trusting in God's great love and mercy, they asked and it was done for them.

In Sirach 35:17-18 we read, "The prayer of the humble pierces the clouds, it does not rest until it reaches its goal nor will it withdraw till the Most High responds." To continue to be used by God it has to be utterly clear to us that our power comes from God and not from ourselves. The more spiritual responsibility we have, the more do we need to humble ourselves.

I read that the late Kathryn Kuhlmann, who was blessed with an extraordinary healing ministry, used to pace back and forth in the wings of the stage before a healing service. Again and again she would pray these words from Psalm 51: "Oh Lord, take not Your Holy Spirit from me." Knowing the needs of the people awaiting her, she was afraid to walk out on that stage without humbling herself before God and begging Him for the anointing of His Holy Spirit. That's humility. God alone is God. We are simply His instruments.

Charles Simpson, a minister, recounts a conversation he had once with the Lord. The Lord said, "Humble yourself, Charles, or I will have to humble you." Charles, a wise disciple, replied, "Knowing what a thorough job You do in such matters, Lord, I'll humble myself!"

There are two ways to "go down." You can humble yourself gracefully, or get knocked down! Personally, I've gone down both ways. Believe me, the graceful way is much easier. Humble yourself! Remember, "pride comes before the fall."

We need to be careful that our prayer does not become that of the "Catholic Pharisee". Have you ever heard that story?

Two Catholics went to church to pray; one was a Catholic Pharisee, the other was not. The Catholic Pharisee with head unbowed prayed in this fashion. "I give you thanks, O God, that I am not like the rest of the Church—confused, half-hearted, rebellious, or even like this ordinary Catholic here. I attend Mass every morning. I'm involved in pastoral leadership. I exercise spiritual gifts. My phone rings constantly because of the wise and learned counsel I dispense. I tithe on all I possess."

The other man, however, kept his distance, not even daring to raise his eyes to heaven. All he did was beat his breast and say, "Oh God, be merciful to me, a sinner." Believe me, this man went home from Church justified and the other did not. For everyone who exalts himself will be humbled while he who humbles himself will be exalted (cf. Luke 18:13-14).

All that we have is a gift from God. Apart from Him we are nothing. To God alone belongs all the praise and honor and glory.

My friends, let's be reminded the foundation of our relationship with God. That foundation is humility—a humility which acknowledges that God is the Creator, and we are the creatures. Let's resolve to humble ourselves in His presence so that our prayers may be heard, that God may do battle for us and that we may be used with power to spread the gospel.

Let's repeat the ejaculation we learned as children, *"Jesus, meek and humble of heart, make our hearts like unto Thine!"*

A Visit to Grandpa's House

Did you ever compare notes with another parent while waiting in a pediatrician's office? It's risky business! Just before Patrick's second birthday, a mom in the doctor's waiting room casually mentioned that her two-year-old had memorized the entire alphabet, could count to ten and construct four word sentences. By contrast, Patrick was still pointing to an object, grunting and waiting for some family member to run and fetch it. On the way home from the doctor's office I sang to Patrick, "A, B, C, D, E, F, G..." hoping he'd catch on and catch up!

Actually, the Lord used Patrick's limited vocabulary soon afterwards to teach me an important lesson. The two of us visited my parents' home in Arizona for a week. Even though Patrick had only seen his grandpa a few times, he quickly fell in love with him. It was a special joy to see the striking resemblance between my father and my child.

But what amazed me the most was how effectively Patrick and his grandpa could communicate while using so few intelligible words. Patrick started a game with my dad. He'd point to him and say, "Grandpa, eat!" Grandpa responded, "Patrick, eat!" Then they'd both start laughing, as if they shared some wonderful secret.

A few days after we arrived, Patrick decided he wanted an even greater closeness to his grandpa. While my dad was slouched down in his favorite chair, feet propped up on an ottoman, Patrick approached. He clambered onto Grandpa's lap and lay down directly on top of him. With his arms embracing Grandpa's chest Patrick looked up lovingly into his eyes. Grandpa gazed down and whispered, "Eat!"

"Eat!" Patrick replied.

Some babbling baby talk followed. The love passing between these two was incredible. I remember feeling grateful to have had Patrick so as to bring my father such pleasure.

Needless to say, Patrick is also our joy and delight!

At one point during our visit, Patrick ran over to my dad, giggling with glee and bent down to kiss Grandpa's bare foot. He wanted to lavish love on Grandpa Gallagher and no sign of affection was beneath his dignity. My dad was deeply moved. "No one has ever loved me like this!" my dad exclaimed.

Now, Mom and I love him tremendously, but we weren't the slightest bit offended. We understood what my dad meant. Patrick, in his childlike simplicity, had touched his grandpa's heart in a unique and powerful way.

Before the visit's end, Patrick got sick and found it painful to swallow. Grandpa suffered along with him, coaxing him to take ice pops and Jello. Patrick's pain was Grandpa's pain. The word "eat" took on a poignant new meaning.

What happened between these two? I'd say it was a beautiful communion. Yet, consider what Patrick did to show his love for Grandpa? He spoke one intelligible word, followed by gibberish and baby talk. He drew near to lean on Grandpa's heart, to gaze into his eyes. He bowed humbly and gladly to kiss Grandpa's foot. He let Grandpa help relieve his pain. Patrick basked in the presence of one who loved him and gratefully returned that love. Just watching these two helped me better understand the simplicity of God's plan for us.

Patrick and my beloved father taught me that our relationship with God doesn't have to be complicated. We don't need fancy words or sophisticated methods to approach our heavenly Father. Pure and simple, God calls us to intimacy with Himself. To gaze on Him. To cling to Him. To speak to Him with our own words and those mysterious words supplied by the Holy Spirit in the gift of tongues. He calls us to honor Him. To eat and be nourished by Him. To let Him comfort us in our pain. To be His reflection to others. To bring joy to His heart.

Yes, Patrick and his grandpa affirm the truth of Jesus' own words: *"Unless you change and become like little children, you shall not enter the Kingdom of God"* (Matthew 18:3).

Had You Turned to Me

"My wife's in excruciating pain with cancer."

"My son left the Church and now he's having an affair."

"My husband is an alcoholic but won't get help. Our family's falling apart."

And these were just her first three people in line at the meeting where my husband and I were ministering! I couldn't bring myself to lift my eyes to see how many more were waiting for prayer. What stories of misery and pain were yet to be disclosed, I wondered? What impossible circumstances would be described? And what could Al and I do anyway? What could we possibly offer?

Then I caught myself. "Wait a minute, Patti. These folks don't need *your* help and advice. They need Jesus, the Master of the Impossible, the One who raises the dead and calls into being things that are not."

That quick reminder put the situation in perspective. For the remainder of the evening I could listen compassionately to my friends' needs, and then place them in the nail-pierced hands of Jesus with confidence. In fact, as Al and I opened ourselves up to the Holy Spirit, we began to receive words from Scripture, exhortations and even prophecies to encourage each person. But the ministry didn't flow out of our own wisdom or resources; it was a gift of the Spirit. When the evening ended, I felt refreshed instead of drained. Turning to Jesus and opening up to the Holy Spirit does that.

I'm not always so quick to turn to Jesus in such situations. One day Al and I went away for a time of rest and prayer at St. Joseph's Abbey, an hour away from our home. We were assisting at Mass when I spotted three people I knew in the congregation. Immediately my heart sank. They were people who usually approached me for ministry. I could just picture my quiet afternoon evaporating in conversation and prayer counseling. My mind began racing for ways to avoid contact with these people after Mass. Although I successfully managed to "escape" conversation, I lost my sense of peace in the process.

Later that day in prayer I recalled the situation and my reaction to it. The Lord seemed to say, "Had you turned to Me immediately, you would have had the grace you needed to respond to them."

Why did I panic? Why did I want to escape? I felt depleted of resources and forgot to turn to the Lord for strength, that's why. I didn't want anyone to interfere with my "private time." By choosing the path of self-reliance and self-protection, I was actually the loser. In that situation I would have found more refreshment by turning to the Lord than by running away.

If you can identify with my desire to escape, take heart! Jesus is accustomed to such reactions from His friends. Remember the Gospel story where the harried disciples, longing to escape from the crowd, retreated to a lonely spot? Imagine their frustration to find that same crowd waiting on the opposite shore! Jesus had compassion on the people "for they were like sheep without a shepherd." And He taught them at great length.

When the disciples tried again for a little privacy by suggesting that Jesus send the crowd away for food, the Lord replied, "You give them something." Then He multiplied the few meager loaves and fish the disciples had given Him, thereby providing enough for everyone, with 12 baskets left to spare!

The lesson is clear: The disciples needed to rely, not on themselves, but on the presence of Jesus, and so do we. *Had you turned to Me immediately.* These words of the Lord remain an invitation and a challenge as I face demands on my time, energy, and love. My resolution is to try to turn to Jesus immediately when I feel like running away so that the words of St. Paul may be my own: *"I can do all things in Him who strengthens me"* (Philippians 4:13).

 **Letting Go**

"Me sad, Mom. Me sad say bye Jim, Ginny, Libba, Michael. Me real sad. You sad, Mom?"

I looked back at my two-and-a-half year old son, Patrick, strapped in his car seat. His bottom lip was quivering.

"Yes, honey, Mommy's sad too." I turned my eyes quickly to the road before he could see they were filled with tears.

We had just said goodbye to our dear friends, the Kellys, who were leaving New Orleans. The huge moving van outside their apartment, the bare walls and packed boxes within made a deep impression on Patrick. So this is what moving means!

How quickly and deeply the Kelly family had worked their way into our hearts and lives. Elizabeth ("Libba" in Patrick-ese) was my son's constant companion. Whether babbling baby talk on the phone, lunching on hot dogs, or learning to share not fight over toys, Patrick and Elizabeth were together. And so were Ginny and I.

"Don't cry, Mom. You cry, me cry. Me sad Libba move." Patrick knew about my tears without seeing my face.

This little guy was getting his first taste of the pain that necessarily comes with loving. How hard it is letting go of those we love!

Of course, I'd been lecturing myself silently for months about the importance of the Kellys' move. But, do you know what?

All my best reasoning didn't remove that pain of separation. Moving day upset me. We can know something is willed or permitted by God, want to embrace it with a generous heart, and still hurt. God's will can be painful. Real loving calls for real dying to self—surrendering—letting go.

As I drove home from the Kellys', Patrick fell asleep. Waiting at a red light my tears flowed freely. "Offer it up," the Holy Spirit reminded me. "Don't waste any suffering, but offer it up in union with Jesus for others." What better response than to unite with Jesus? Surely His human and Sacred Heart understands such pain. Did He not weep at the tomb of Lazarus? Did He not long for the companionship of His friends in the Garden of Gethsemani? I found myself thinking with greater compassion about others who have struggled to "let go" recently.

Take my friend Melanie who has just sent two children off to college. The nest is getting empty. While she rejoices in their independence, she misses them terribly. Nothing seemed to console her until she turned to the Lord for the grace to let go.

A greater letting go has been required of Nancy and Chick. Their 23-year-old son Dean was killed instantly in a car accident. In the midst of their pain they wrote their friends, "Through this tragedy we have come to know that relationships are the most important things in our lives: First our relationship with God, then with family, friends and others. If we had not told Dean often that we loved him, if we had not hugged him, we could not do it now. Dean knew we loved him and we know he loved us."

What words of wisdom! We should cherish those around us in the present moment. Each person is a gift to be treasured while we can. We don't know yet how we may have to let go this coming year, but we do know that Jesus Our Lord will be there for us in every circumstance.

Hidden within the pain of each letting go is a call to cling to Jesus more closely than ever. All other relationships, all other loves are passing. *God alone* endure forever.

Let's determine to hold fast to Jesus, to draw consolation and strength from Jesus in each letting go, so that we may experience *His* peace which surpasses understanding. Friends may move, children will grow up and leave home, loved ones are taken from us in death. Yet our hearts can be at peace. For remember God has said, *"I will never desert you, nor will I forsake you"* (Hebrews 13:6).

Welcome!

Welcome! Bienvenue! Benvenidos!

These words of greeting can be found scrawled across billboards and buses all over our city. As a "tourist town" New Orleans is anxious to extend a gracious welcome to visitors. We want people to return to our city, and so our parting words are," Ya'll come back, ya hear!"

Hospitality, that art of making guests feel welcome and comfortable, is a marvelous gift. Recently we visited the home of some friends who treated my family like royalty. Ever since we first met these folks, they've been inviting us to visit, and when we did, our time was truly a joy. They made us feel right at home and urged us to stay longer next time. Being welcomed in such a manner makes a person want to return. I've found that the opposite is also true: It's a relief to leave a place where you feel like an intruder.

The art of hospitality applies to our own relationship with God as well. In 1967 I attended a retreat with students from Duquesne University in Pittsburgh, Pennsylvania and we invited the Holy Spirit to visit us with His power and gifts. We welcomed Him, even though we didn't understand all that it would mean. Over and over again we prayed, "Come Holy Spirit!" And the Holy Spirit *did* come in a deeper and more manifest way than ever before.

In a great outpouring of love, the Holy Spirit has been coming all over the face of the earth these many years since, and He's not finished yet! The Spirit of our mighty and sovereign Lord is still coming! There is so much more He wishes to accomplish in our world. God's Spirit is still coming in power to those who will receive Him. But herein lies the key question: Will we graciously welcome the visitation of the Holy Spirit or treat Him as an intruder?

I believe the Charismatic Renewal has spread widely in the past few decades because of men and women who have welcomed the action of the Holy Spirit. There's been a price to pay. It's called "the cost of Pentecost". Remember, it always takes self-sacrifice to welcome a guest. Yet those who have been willing to forego their own plans in order to embrace God's plan have been mightily used by the Holy Spirit. Such men and women have become fathers and mothers to countless spiritual children.

Welcoming the Holy Spirit requires great generosity but brings great rewards. In lives that are open to His visitation, the Spirit is a source of continual refreshment as we read in the "Sequence Hymn for Pentecost":

Thou, of comforters the best;
Thou, the soul's most welcome guest;
Sweet refreshment here below.

Comfort, light, peace, and joy come with His visit. How God's Spirit must delight in those who never tire of welcoming Him no matter what the circumstances. He wants to return to such as these, for in them He can be at home.

Unfortunately, it is all too easy to resist the action of the Holy Spirit—to quench and stifle, to grieve and even reject the Spirit of the living God. We are not always welcoming hosts. Rather, our attitude is often one of fear and caution. We don't want the bother of having a guest. We say to the Holy Spirit, "Don't come now; it's inconvenient. Don't enter this area; it's off limits. Don't touch that; it's one of my prized possessions. Don't ask such a question; it makes me uncomfortable. Don't expect so much; I've given enough. Don't give me that gift; it doesn't suit my taste."

We all know of people in the Church who cannot accept the way God has worked in the Charismatic Renewal. But there are also people in the Charismatic Renewal who have stopped welcoming the action of the Holy Spirit. At some point they closed the door. God gives us a wonderful yet terrible freedom in relating to Him. The choice is ours, to welcome or resist the continued visitation of the Holy Spirit.

Let's resolve to put out the welcome mat once again! Let's invite the Holy Spirit to come anew and be our soul's "most welcome guest." Let's offer no resistance to His action. May He have freedom to clean house, rearrange furniture, tear down walls or add another room—whatever He wills. In the words of a hymn to the Holy Spirit we say, "Melt us! Mold us! Fill us! Use us!"

Daily my husband and I invoke the Holy Spirit by praying the Sequence Hymn of Pentecost and the *Veni Creator Spiritus*. I include it here with a word of encouragement. Please don't allow the Holy Spirit to become the "Forgotten Person" of the Trinity in your life. Pray to Him daily and you will come to know His sweet abiding presence.

Sequence Hymn of Pentecost

Come, Thou Holy Spirit, come;
And from Thy celestial home
Shed a ray of light divine;

Come, Thou Father of the poor;
Come, Thou source of all our store;
Come, within our bosoms shine;

Thou, of comforters the best;
Thou, the soul's most welcome guest;
Sweet refreshment here below;

In our labor, rest most sweet;
Grateful coolness in the heat;
Solace in the midst of woe.

O most blessed Light divine,
Shine within these hearts of Thine,
And our inmost being fill;

Where Thou are not, man hath naught,
Nothing good in deed or thought,
Nothing free from taint of ill.

Heal our wounds, our strength renew;
On our dryness pour Thy dew;
Wash the stains of guilt away;

Bend the stubborn heart and will;
Melt the frozen, warm the chill;
Guide the steps that go astray.

On the faithful, who adore
And confess Thee, evermore
In Thy sev'nfold gift descend;

Give them virtue's sure reward;
Give them Thy salvation, Lord;
Give them joys that never end.

Amen. Alleluia.

Veni Creator Spiritus

Come, O Creator Spirit blest!
And in our souls take up Thy rest;
Come, with Thy grace and heav'nly aid,
To fill the hearts which Thou hast made.

Great Paraclete! to Thee we cry;
O highest gift of God most high!
O fount of life! O fire of love!
And sweet anointing from above!

Thou dost appear in sev'nfold dow'r
The sign of God's almighty pow'r!
The Father's promise, making rich
With saving truth our earthly speech.

Kindle our senses from above,
And make our hearts o'erflow with love;
With patience firm and virtue high,
The weakness of our flesh supply.

Far from us drive the foe we dread,
And grant us Thy true peace instead;
So shall we not, with Thee for guide.
Turn from the path of life aside.

O may Thy grace on us bestow
The Father and the Son to know,
And Thee, through endless times confessed,
Of Both th' eternal Spirit blest.

All glory, while the ages run,
Be to the Father and the Son
Who rose from death: the same to Thee,
O Holy Ghost, eternally.

Amen.

The Least of the Gifts?

"Did you realize you were just praying in perfect French?" I asked in surprise.

"No," came the reply. "Was I?"

Having studied French I understood the beautiful words of praise my friend had just uttered in tongues. We were both newly baptized in the Holy Spirit at the time. How our sense of awe and wonder increased as we realized that God had enabled my friend to praise Him in a new language.

I've never understood why the gift of tongues is referred to as "the least" of the spiritual gifts. Perhaps this terminology comes from the passage in which St. Paul says that the one who prophesies is greater than the one who speaks in tongues (II Corinthians 14:5). Maybe some people conclude that the gift of tongues is less valuable because it's mentioned towards the end of the list of spiritual gifts (II Corinthians 12:7-11). While it may be true that in the assembly there are other gifts that contribute more directly to building up the Church, the gift of tongues is an invaluable aid for personal prayer.

Of course, I didn't always realize this myself. At first I neither understood nor desired this gift. After the Baptism in the Holy Spirit I was able to pray in English with new freedom and joy. I wondered why it was necessary to have another prayer language. But before very long I began to feel the need for greater power in my praise and greater understanding of God's mind in my intercession. Because there was no one to explain to me that yielding to tongues is a matter of speaking out in faith with one's own voice, I waited in silence day after day for a new language to overtake me.

One day I woke up with a clicking in my throat. I cut my classes for fear that this charism would burst forth from my mouth and embarrass me. (That is not the way it works, by the way!) I retreated to an oratory above the chapel at Duquesne and knelt in front of a crucifix. I said to Jesus, "I am not getting up from my knees until I pray in tongues." And I waited with my mouth open. When I finally yielded to the gift of tongues, it came forth as a beautiful song of praise. Though I did not recognize the language, in my spirit I sensed I was singing Mary's *Magnificat*. From that day on I have been convinced that I am better equipped to praise God and serve others because of the gift of tongues.

One striking example of this occurred years ago. I was awakened in the middle of the night by a sense that I should intercede for something very serious. Not knowing the nature of the need, I began to pray in tongues. As I prayed a heaviness came upon my spirit and I labored for a long time interceding in tongues for this unknown situation. Finally, the prayer burden lifted and I went back to sleep.

The next day I discovered that my family had been in a terrible car accident in another state at the very time God called me to prayer. They had been miraculously spared any injury. In fact, the policeman on the scene said, "God had to be with you to come through this accident unharmed." The Lord enabled me through the gift of tongues to intercede for my family's safety. If the gift of tongues had helped me in this situation alone I would be eternally grateful for it. But experiences like this have occurred in my life time and again.

Not only for personal needs, but for the needs of the Church and the world, we are called to steadfast intercession. The gift of tongues can help make us strong prayer warriors who can win victories in the Spirit for God's people.

If you have already received this precious gift, stir it up and use it! Be open to receiving a new profusion of tongues and new languages. My husband prays in a new gift of tongues frequently. If you have not received the gift of tongues, then seek it! Ask others to lay hands on you and pray that you may yield to this wonderful gift of prayer! It's yours for the asking! No gift of God is to be disdained or ignored whether it is called "the greatest" or "the least." Praying in tongues has strengthened my relationship with Jesus and helped me intercede for His people. Never shall I call it the least of His gracious gifts.

The Quality of Mercy

The quality of mercy is not strain'd,
It droppeth as the gentle rain from heaven
Upon the place beneath: it is twice blest;
It blesseth him that gives and him that takes...

As a high school student I memorized these lines from
Shakespeare's *The Merchant of Venice*. But it was only later,
in surrendering my life to Jesus as Lord, that I began to
understand something about that "quality of mercy."

As we receive God's mercy, so we are called to show forth that
mercy to others. Part of the transforming work of the Holy
Spirit is to teach us how to do that. This was brought home to
me by the following experience.

Before I was married, I shared an apartment with several
other Christian women. One day one of the young women
asked to borrow my car to visit her sister. Although I had
loaned her my car before, I was very hesitant on this occasion.
It was raining hard and I was afraid for her safety and for my
car. I told her that it would be unwise to drive alone in such
a storm and that I'd prefer for her to wait. But she felt it was
important to go immediately, and so she did.

Some hours later I was eating dinner when she returned. I can
still see her standing in the doorway looking very ashamed.
"Patti, I got in a wreck on the bridge and your car had to be
towed away."

In a flash, I knew what mercy was. In my mind's eye I could see myself getting up from the table and embracing her with these words, "Thank God you weren't hurt. It's all right. Don't worry about it." In fact, I believe the Lord was offering me the grace to respond in just that way.

But quickly following this impulse of mercy, reason intervened. I thought to myself, "Why should I console her? After all, she wrecked my car. I told her to postpone her trip. It's not reasonable to let her go without some kind of reproach."

I looked at her sullenly and finally mumbled something like, "I told you it wasn't the best time to go."

Meekly she left the room. There I sat at the table alone knowing I had missed an opportunity to be merciful as my heavenly Father is merciful. At a later time she and I could have discussed the implications of the accident. In that moment, however, the merciful thing would have been to console her.

His ways are not our ways. His thoughts are not our thoughts. Mercy will never "make sense" or seem "reasonable." The prodigal son deserved a reproach. Instead his merciful father welcomed him with a loving embrace. This is divine folly. God always deals with us out of the abundance of His mercy. We can rejoice that our Lord never gives us what we truly deserve.

Let's pray that we can yield to the Holy Spirit when He prompts us to be merciful. Then the words of Jesus may rightly apply to us: *"Blessed are the merciful, for they shall obtain mercy"* (Matthew 5:7).

 Fantastic!

"Mom, why do I have to wait two more years to receive my First Holy Communion?"

This was the question my six-year-old son, Peter, asked me. When I inquired as to why he was so anxious to receive Communion his answer was simple. "I want to receive Jesus. I want my sins taken away and I want more of the Holy Spirit. My heart is ready, Mom! My heart is ready!" By his beautiful answer, so full of faith, I was convinced that Peter was indeed ready. Without having read the psalms, the Spirit of God within him was echoing the words of King David from long ago, "My heart is ready, O God, my heart is ready" (Psalm 57:8).

My husband decided to approach our pastor and ask for permission. But my son couldn't wait. After Mass on Sunday, Peter, who is usually shy, went up to the pastor himself. "Father, may I please have permission to receive my First Holy Communion soon?" To my amazement the pastor said, "Yes, I'm sure your Mom and Dad have been preparing you. It's good that you had the courage to ask for yourself." Our son Peter is taking the Kingdom of God by storm!

In this time of preparation, Peter and I have had many wonderful conversations about Jesus and the sacraments. Although I thought I would be the teacher, I am learning so much from him instead. I explained to Peter how Jesus forgives us when we repent. The Bible says that though our sins be as scarlet (that's bright red, I explained) God will make them white as snow. When we go to Confession, it is Jesus Himself waiting for us in the person of the priest. He is anxious to forgive us and take all our sins away. Peter looked at me in amazement. "You mean it's like He throws them in the garbage? Then they're gone forever?! That's *fantastic*!."

"Yes, son," I replied, "That is *fantastic*."

As we shared more about the Eucharist, I used the image of Jesus looking for a place to be born. Our hearts, small and limited, are like the stable in Bethlehem. I told Peter, "It's Jesus Himself, who now wants to find a place in your heart." Once again that look of wonder spread across his face. "You mean God will really be living in my body? Mom, that's *fantastic!*"

St. Augustine put it this way. "God became man so that man might become God." Though we remain creatures, we share in His divine life. Jesus became poor that we might become rich. St. Paul writes, "Truly great is the mystery of our religion" (I Timothy 3:16). The little saint who lives in our home says simply, "*That's fantastic!*" There is an appreciation, a sense of wonder and gratitude for the gift of life in Christ Jesus.

Peter's response to the mysteries of our faith is teaching me not to take for granted these sacraments of our salvation. The mercy of Jesus is waiting for us in the Sacrament of Reconciliation. The love of Jesus is there when we share in His Body and Blood. How often do we enter into intimate contact with Jesus and yet fail to recognize the gift we have received? Do we limit the transforming power of the Lord in the sacraments because we are not eager and full of faith?

Jesus tells us, "Unless you become like little children you shall not enter the Kingdom of heaven" (Matthew 18:3). Peter is counting the days until he can be one with Jesus. As his First Communion day approaches, I pray that the Lord may renew in all of us the simplicity of children who know how to marvel at the Father's gracious gifts. And may we too learn to say, "It's *fantastic!*"

PS.   Peter's son, John, is now preparing to receive his First Holy Communion shortly. *That's fantastic!*

The Joy of Repentance

My son, Mark, had a wonderful first-grade teacher. She was loving but firm, and in her class Mark really began to enjoy learning. Unfortunately, in the middle of the year she had to move.

The children were very disappointed. No one could ever take their teacher's place. With the energy only seven-year-olds can muster, the children devised ways to let their new teacher know they didn't like the change.

One day Mark came home with a note saying that he had to be punished because of misbehavior in class. In his own defense, Mark explained that he wasn't the only one to be punished; six boys were sent to the office for giving the new teacher a hard time that day. Mark figured that going to the office in a group was less serious than going alone! His dad and I thought otherwise.

Mark had been a good student and a cooperative child in class until this incident. Both my husband and I had taught school, so we tried to help Mark understand his teacher's point of view.

"It's hard for a teacher to come into a class so late in the school year. She really needs your help, Mark," my husband explained. "As punishment, I'm going to give you an assignment.

Al continued, "Tomorrow when you get to class, I want you to go up to your teacher and apologize for your behavior. Tell her you're sorry and that you'll try to do better."

Poor Mark! He pleaded with his dad to change his mind. None of the other boys would have to apologize.

"Do anything, Dad, but please don't make me tell the teacher I'm sorry," Mark cried. But Al held firm.

The next day Mark left for school with a scowl on his face, but he came home with a smile. With joy, he told me that after he apologized to his teacher, she not only forgave him, but put her arms around him and planted a kiss on his cheek. He still had the lipstick there to prove it!

"You know, Mom, at first I felt afraid, then I felt embarrassed. But after I said I was sorry, I felt really happy!"

In fact, Mark's joy was so genuine that he had gone to his other teachers to ask for their forgiveness as well. One of his teachers was surprised. "But, Mark, you've never done anything wrong in my class." He just wanted to make sure. Repenting felt so good; once Mark started he didn't want to stop.

That night Mark told everyone at the dinner table how the lipstick got on his cheek. "Now I want everybody in the whole family to forgive me for doing anything wrong to any of you." Needless to say, there were many more hugs and kisses for Mark.

Repentance brings joy. It's that simple. Let's be quick to repent and ask forgiveness when we need to so that our joy may be full.

Stir It Up!

My dear friend, Fr. Jim Ferry, told me about one of the shortest and most powerful testimonies he ever heard concerning the Baptism in the Holy Spirit. It came from the lips of Capuchin Fr. Raniero Cantalamessa, the Preacher to the Papal Household. Fr. Cantalamessa said simply this: "I had two lives; one before the Baptism in the Holy Spirit, and one after."

And it's just that simple and that powerful! The Baptism in the Holy Spirit is meant to be a life-changing experience. As my friend, Fr. Harold Cohen, SJ, puts it: "At the age of 40, I knelt down and asked some college kid to pray over me for the Baptism in the Holy Spirit. All I felt was foolish. But my life has never been the same since. 'Life begins at 40' describes it for me."

I heard that a theology professor laughingly told his students he was going to give them a sophisticated theological description of the Baptism in the Holy Spirit. "Take out your pens and write this: *It's a big grace!*" While there *are* real theological descriptions of this "big grace", most of us who have been baptized in the Holy Spirit aren't equipped to give them. But what we *do* have is an experiential knowledge of a new power, a new peace, a new joy in the Lord. Catholic Christian life is different than before.

I have some friends who came up with a wonderful analogy to describe the Baptism in the Holy Spirit from a recent experience in their lives. For years they'd noticed that the parts to their used car were unusually expensive. Then one day they learned that this vehicle had within it a police interceptor engine, more powerful than they'd ever imagined. A few weeks later, my friend was on the road alone when a seedy looking character in a truck pulled up alongside her car at a red light. For miles he kept tailing her close, then taunting her by pulling next to her. She felt uneasy and threatened until it dawned on her that she had within that car the very power she needed. All she had to do was use it. When the light turned green, she floored the gas pedal and that police interceptor engine propelled her to safety. Her taunter's truck was a tiny speck in the rear view mirror in no time flat. Sweet victory!

When she got home and told her husband, a light went on for him. "It's just like we experienced with the Baptism in the Holy Spirit. The power was there all along." And he was right.

You see, we already have the Holy Spirit within us by virtue of the sacraments of Baptism and Confirmation. But we need to have that power unleashed. When we pray to be baptized in the Holy Spirit, we're asking for a release of the power already present. When we're open to a new fullness of the Spirit's power, we have more of God's grace operating in and through us. We're filled with joy and want everyone to know the reason why. It's God! As St. Paul writes in Ephesians 3:20, "Glory be to Him whose power (that's the Spirit) working in us can do *infinitely* more than we can ask or imagine."

My friend, Fr. Cohen, saw a description of the Baptism in the Holy Spirit while preparing a glass of chocolate milk one night. A fellow Jesuit held out a glass of milk and Fr. Cohen poured in some Hershey's chocolate syrup. Naturally, all the syrup went straight to the bottom of the glass. Fr. Cohen said to his friend, "You've got to stir it up." Then it dawned on him. That's the Baptism in the Holy Spirit! The Holy Spirit is already present, poured out, so to speak, but you've got to stir it up. If it's not stirred up, the Hershey's syrup remains at the bottom and the milk is without flavor. But if you stir it up, a transformation takes place—everything tastes better than before.

How greatly our Lord is longing to grant us a fresh outpouring of His Holy Spirit. Listen to His promise from Scripture: "And I tell you, ask and it shall be given you; seek, and you will find. Knock and it will be opened to you. For everyone who asks receives, and he who seeks finds, and to him who knocks it will be opened. What father among you if his son asks for a fish will instead of a fish give him a serpent; or if he asks for an egg, will give him a scorpion? If you then, who are evil, know how to give good gifts to your children, how much more will the heavenly Father give the Holy Spirit to those that ask Him!" (Luke 11:9-13). *How much more! How much more!* Our heavenly Father will not deny His Holy Spirit to those who ask.

This "big grace," this "police interceptor engine," this "chocolate syrup"—the Baptism in the Holy Spirit—is available to everyone! Ask Jesus to be Lord and Master of your life. Ask your heavenly Father to release within you the power of the Holy Spirit in Jesus' name. Ask others to lay hands on you and pray for the charismatic gifts to begin to flow through you to build up the Body of Christ, the Church,

Please, please, I beg you, don't miss out on the grace, the power, the refreshment waiting for you in the Baptism in the Holy Spirit! Ask and you shall receive!

# The Prayer Room

Every year our prayer group is involved in hosting the Southern Regional Conference of the Catholic Charismatic Renewal. I have come to love this yearly gathering. It's a privilege to come together with several thousand Catholic Charismatics to praise and worship, to be taught, and to see the Lord act with power.

No matter how outstanding the message of the conference is, there is always something else that manages to touch me. It is the generosity and commitment of the volunteers who work at the conference. Hundreds of people each year pledge their time and talents to serve.

One of my children asked me recently what these workers get paid for their service. He was shocked to find out there is no monetary reward for the countless hours of work they do. Instead, they find their joy in being like their Master who said, "I am among you as one who serves" (Matthew 20:28). In the words of one of the men who constructs the stage, "I'd rather do this job for the Lord than make a million dollars!"

Several years ago I was particularly struck by the beauty of one of the conference volunteers named Ethel. She had been recommended to serve in the Word Gift Unit. This group is comprised of brothers and sisters from various prayer groups who have tested gifts of prophecy, exhortation and revelation. They come together in prayer before each conference session. Then they are seated on stage to minister through the operation of the word gifts. It is a great responsibility to serve in such a way, and it is also a real honor.

When Ethel was invited to be part of this group she set about seeking God's will. Although she was willing to serve in the Word Gift Unit, she wanted to be sure this was exactly where the Lord wanted her during the conference. After a time of prayer, Ethel discerned that she should be part of the Prayer Room team instead. During meal breaks at the conference, people with special needs come to the prayer room to receive ministry. There, hidden away in a corner of the prayer room, the Lord used Ethel to manifest His glory in a dramatic way.

Many people came to Ethel for prayer. According to the light God gave, Ethel prayed for each one's needs. Finally, a tiny Vietnamese woman approached her. As she came forward, the Holy Spirit prompted Ethel to remove her shoes with the sense that she was standing on holy ground. The little lady stood before Ethel with her hands joined in prayer and bowed low from the waist. In the next few moments it was clear that the Vietnamese woman could neither speak nor understand English. Ethel knew no Vietnamese.

Because of the circumstances Ethel relied on the gift of tongues in her intercession for this sister's needs. As Ethel prayed she soon realized that she was no longer praying in the tongue she usually used. Instead, the Holy Spirit gave her a new language—one that sounded like Vietnamese! Ethel soon became convinced that she was indeed praying in Vietnamese when the tiny lady began to converse with her in the same language. You can imagine the sense of awe that came upon them in those moments!

When they finished praying, the Vietnamese woman bowed low to Ethel, and Ethel returned this beautiful, reverent gesture. The little lady walked away having received ministry in the power of the Holy Spirit. God had reached down and touched her, despite the language barrier.

Ethel was thrilled! How grateful she was to be in the prayer room at that moment so that God could use her. Had she accepted the invitation to serve in the Word Gift Unit, her service would have been more visible. But the Lord was calling her to be hidden in humble service where she could be His instrument in this special way.

I have seen this same spirit of humility and obedience in countless others whose hearts are set on serving the Lord. They have no concern for their own glory. They desire the glory of their Master. I thank God for men and women like these who listen to and obey His voice. May the Lord Himself reward them for their humble service!

Just for Jesus

When Sr. Isabel Bettwy visited me recently and she met three-year-old Patrick, he kept whispering in my ear, "Tell your sister about my cowboy boots. Tell your sister about my cowboy hat." I tried to explain to him that Sr. Isabel isn't exactly my sister. She's a religious sister.

"Where's Sistersbel's children?" Patrick asked.

"She doesn't have children of her own," I responded, hoping my answer would satisfy him. No such luck with a three-year-old!

"How come?"

At this point, handling the traditional toddler question, "Why is the sky blue, Mommy?", would have been a snap compared to explaining celibacy in three-year-old terminology. It's moments like these when I'm sure the Lord must chuckle as He sends the Holy Spirit out to rescue flustered parents.

"Patrick, Sr. Isabel doesn't have her own husband or children. She's—she's—'just for Jesus'. (Those words popped into my head.) Jesus wants her to belong to Him in a special way so she can be a sister to everyone."

This "just for Jesus" idea had a catchy ring to it. Since I had just read an article about planting the seeds of priestly vocation in the young, I decided to seize the moment.

"Patrick, you know Fr. Cohen? He's a priest. He's just for Jesus.

And Fr. Lafranz? He's just for Jesus too. And someday if you become a priest, you'll be..." But before I could finish the sentence with my brilliant "just for Jesus," Patrick interrupted.

"Me no want to be priest! Me want to be cowboy! With boots and a horse and a rope and a gun! Me no want to be priest, Mom!" He was glaring at me by now. For Patrick there was no problem giving up wife and family, just don't touch his horse or saddle!

So much for planting the seeds of a priestly vocation in my sons, I mused. But to my surprise, soon afterwards I found myself talking about the priesthood with my teenage son. While I was giving him a haircut, he told me about someone he knew. Although this young man always imagined that marriage would be his vocation, he's now beginning to wonder about the priesthood. "How do you know if you're called?", my son asked.

I tried to explain that every young person has to come before the Lord with an open, generous heart to discern his vocation. "If God is calling you to serve Him in marriage, that will bring you true happiness. But if God is calling you to the priesthood, then it's being a priest that will bring you fulfillment."

"If that's true, Mom, why do so many priests seem unhappy?", my teenager asked in great earnestness. Patrick's questions suddenly seemed easy, compared to this one!

"Son, I'm no expert, but it might be that some priests seem unhappy because they're not praying as they should. I don't mean they've stopped saying prayers. I mean they may not be taking delight in the Lord and communicating with Him from the heart. If a priest doesn't have that deep union with Jesus, he won't be very happy in his priest hood. Then there's the loneliness. If God is inviting someone to be a priest, he needs to find the support and friendship of others."

Haircut finished. End of conversation. But not the end of my thoughts. These two sons of mine have made me ponder anew the priestly vocation. Being "just for Jesus." Belonging exclusively to God to be fruitful for His people. Delighting in the Lord in prayer. Finding the right support and fellowship to sustain life.

Priesthood. "One does not take this honor on his own initiative, but only when called by God as Aaron was" (Hebrew 5:4). How much our priests need loving support to remain faithful to this life of discipleship and service! Let's commit ourselves to support our priests by serious intercession for them. The Lord promises, *"I will lavish choice portions on the priests, that My people shall be filled with My goodness"* (Jeremiah 31:14). Let's pray that the Lord will do this today and grant them a tremendous renewal in the Holy Spirit.

 # Honor Thy Mother

I am blessed with a lovely mother. Far beyond the nine months she carried me and the early years she cared for me, her love has nourished my life. She is to me not only a mother, but also a dear friend and sister in the Lord. In fact, there is no other woman I admire more than my own mother, Netta Gallagher.

How well I remember my mother's visit after the birth of our second child. She cooked, cleaned and gave lots of encouragement. "Your mother is such a loving person," commented my husband one day. "She really has a servant's heart. Now I see for myself why you think she's special." I was happy that two people I loved so much were coming to know and love each other as well. A lesson was beginning to unfold for me.

Mother's birthday occurred during her visit. In the midst of baby preparations I had neglected to buy her a gift. My husband bought her something, but I felt badly that I had nothing to give her myself. There was little I could do to serve her for she was serving me.

But when her birthday arrived something wonderful happened. Two of my friends, without a word from me, remembered her birthday. One prepared a delicious meal and delivered it piping hot. The other brought her a beautiful card and gift. These friends had already cooked for me and given me gifts. Now they were honoring my mother.

Mother was amazed. "Why are your friends doing this when they hardly know me?" she asked. Then she answered her own question. "It must be out of love for you." To be sure, love for my mother was love for me. Honor for her was really honor for me. How grateful I was to my friends for honoring my mother! How much more I loved them for loving her! They had come to know her through my words. Now they were entering into a relationship with her because of me and this brought me great joy.

Quite suddenly I was caught up in the relationship of another mother and child. I understood in a new way how love for the mother of Jesus takes nothing away from love for Jesus Himself. From the cross the Lord said to the beloved disciple, "Behold your mother," and the disciple received Mary into his home. Out of love for Him, the friends of Jesus still receive her today.

The more we come to Mary and experience her help in our lives, the more we love her. We begin to cherish in Mary those very qualities that made her "blessed among women." As we love and honor her, we are also loving and honoring her Son. We choose her as mother because God chose her as mother.

It's because of Jesus that we enter into a relationship with Mary. Just as my love for my friends increased when they honored my mother as their own, so does Jesus' love for us abound when we honor His mother Mary as our own. The Lord commands us, "Honor thy mother." I rejoice to know I am pleasing God when I honor both my mother on earth and my mother in heaven.

Take Off Your Shoes

I have a confession to make. I love to go around the house barefoot. Always have. Always will. My shoes can be found in various locations—next to the living room rocker, under the kitchen table, by the sewing machine—anywhere but on my feet! My children know this too.

"What are you doing with your shoes on, Mom?" asked my three-year-old son, Patrick, one day.

He looked surprised and apprehensive. I had been away from him for several days and he was afraid I'd leave again. "Take off your shoes, Mom," he pleaded. "Here, I'll help you. Please take off your shoes."

As he bent over me to unfasten my sandals, I looked at him with love. It's so difficult for little ones to understand why we sometimes have to leave them. I tried to give Patrick plenty of tender loving care for the next few days to assure him of his place in my heart. On his part, he showered me with hugs and kisses galore. He loves me. He needs me.

I don't know about you, but I find it a struggle to balance the various demands on my time and attention. There's family, friends, school functions, work, apostolic activity, correspondence, social obligations. The list never ends. No wonder many women, especially those who work outside the home as well as within it, find themselves "stressed out."

In the midst of such tensions in my own life, I've found it helpful to pray to the Holy Spirit. Remember the song, "Let it breathe on me, let the breath of God now breathe on me?" We who are mothers of young families desperately need the breath of God to breathe on us today! Not only do we need the wisdom, light and discernment of the Holy Spirit, we also need great courage to live in the midst of a society that devalues the vocation and ministry of motherhood.

This notion of motherhood as a ministry is one of the lights the Holy Spirit sent me to help discern my own priorities. It was a young mother from Texas who opened up this reality to me. She said, "The Holy Spirit has taught me that I have a ministry of motherhood. In the past, I always loved my three children, but I never thought of them as my ministry. I used to dream about the day they'd be grown and I could do something important for God. Now I realize that being mother to these children right now is in itself a ministry." Her priorities became clearer once she realized the value God places on her relationships in the home.

Another young mother came to me recently for discernment. She has a one-year-old baby whom she's breastfeeding, and she works twenty hours a week as a nurse. "Am I doing enough for God?" she asked. Enough?! I shared with her about the ministry of motherhood and assured her that Jesus was pleased with the service she was already rendering Him. She needn't search for something more spiritual or important!

One January as I mapped out my schedule and responsibilities for the new year it was clear that I could not take on even one additional commitment. Across the top of the page I wrote, "*think no!*" Sometimes it's necessary to "*think no*" because you're committed to the ministry of motherhood. Do you accept that promotion at work, knowing it will mean more hours away from home? Do you chair that committee, even if it conflicts with your child's music lessons? Do you undertake this personal project at a time of special need in the family? Choices must be made.

As I invoke the Holy Spirit over my very busy life, I hear Patrick's words echoing in my heart. "Take off your shoes, Mom." It's reminiscent of God's word to Moses, isn't it? "Take off your shoes, for the ground on which you stand is holy." I believe that we who have chosen the ministry of motherhood will also discover God's holy presence in the midst of family life. Though the angels surrounding us at home may have dirty faces, we too are standing on holy ground.

But Without Love

There are probably few Scripture passages better known and loved than the famous one from I Corinthians 13. This beautiful commentary on love by St. Paul is chosen by many a bride and groom for their wedding liturgy. I don't know about you, but I can never read this passage without squirming a bit. Who among us does not need to grow in the greatest of all virtues—love?

I've heard effective teachings on I Corinthians 13 where the personality of Jesus is described using this famous passage. Have you ever been told to substitute the name of Jesus every time you see the word "love" in I Corinthians 13:4-8? For instance, "Jesus is patient and kind. Jesus is not jealous, or boastful; He is not arrogant or rude. Jesus does not insist on His own way; He is not irritable or resentful; He does not rejoice at wrong but rejoices in the right—Jesus never fails."

Because we're called to be transformed into the image of Jesus, it's then recommended we substitute our own names in the place of His. For example, "Patti is patient; Patti is kind." That's as far as I get. Along with mothers throughout the world, I feel it will take a lifetime to fulfill even that first description where my name is equated with patience!

How well I remember the first time this passage on love came alive to me. It was shortly after I was baptized in the Holy Spirit and I was working at a summer job. After a full day at work and a long bus ride home, I went to a parish prayer meeting. After the meeting which ended rather late everyone was gathered in small groups. I was giving a presentation about the Baptism in the Holy Spirit when suddenly a woman interrupted me with a question. There was just something about this woman, her manner and question, that irritated me. It was late and I was tired. All I wanted was to finish my talk, go home and go to bed. Here was this woman detaining me with her silly question. Despite my irritation, I managed to give her a fairly good answer. In fact, it seemed as though my ears were hearing what my mouth was saying. I felt the Holy Spirit was giving me specific guidance as to what to say. When the meeting finally ended, I was grateful to leave.

But the Holy Spirit had a lesson to teach the teacher. In the middle of the night I was awakened with the words of I Corinthians 13:1-3 ringing in my mind. "If I speak in the tongues of men and of angels, but have not love, I am a noisy gong or a clanging cymbal. And if I have prophetic powers, and understand all mysteries and all knowledge, and if I have all faith, so as to remove mountains, but have not love, I am nothing. If I give away all I have, and if I deliver my body to be burned, but have not love, I gain nothing."

In a flashback I saw myself relating to that woman. I saw my impatience and irritability. The Holy Spirit communicated to me something like this. "Your answer tonight was right, but you were wrong. You spoke without love. You gained nothing, it profited you nothing, you were nothing, without love." Because my service was not rendered in love even if I spoke the truth, I had not served well. The answer was right but the attitude was wrong. I had come under conviction.

This is one of the most wonderful things that happens when we're baptized in the Holy Spirit. The Lord loves us too much to tolerate sin, selfishness or bad attitudes in our lives. If we're serious about growing in holiness, He will teach us how we need to change. And there's no escaping the purifying fire of the word of God!

In everything we say and do we're called to show forth the love of Jesus Christ. That's our vocation as Christians. Such love commands attention. It has transforming power. In our own time we have the example of Blessed Mother Teresa of Calcutta and Pope Saint John Paul II. The love of Christ impelled them to reach out to millions of people with the gospel. Even though they ministered to multitudes, they never lost sight of the dignity and beauty of each individual person.

During the papal visit in 1987, the people of New Orleans shared a common impression of our Pope Saint John Paul II. From the Archbishop in the St. Louis Cathedral to the teenagers in the Superdome, each one of us felt the Pope's personal love. His warmth, his tone of voice, his words, his touch, all communicated this message: "You are special to God and special to me. You are loved." Even an unbelieving world takes notice of such love!

Let's renew our relationship with Jesus who is Love. Only deep union with the Lord Jesus can produce in us the kind of love which "bears all things, believes all things, hopes all things and endures all things" (I Corinthians 13:7). May this love be the root and foundation of our lives so that whatever we say, whatever we do, we may be instruments of His wonderful love.

 # The Things that Really Matter

Recently the mail contained an advertisement which caught my eye. It pictured a large, warmly-lit home against a darkened sky. Across the top of the page were these words:

Because you care about the things that really matter.

Unfolding the ad, I found colorful graphics describing a new magazine featuring the "down home values" of small towns across America. The publication promised to warm the hearts of those who cared about life's most important things.

Although I didn't subscribe to the magazine, its catchy phrase about "the things that really matter" reminded me of a significant dream I had had years ago. I dreamt I was going back home to Irvington, New Jersey, the town where I grew up.

In the dream, my husband and children were with me, and I was anxious to show them the place where I used to live. As we approached the familiar corner building that housed three apartments and two stores, I pointed it out to my children. This was the place of so many happy childhood memories. From the outside, it looked like it always did, but I was greatly surprised when I opened the door!

Instead of finding the hallway and stairs that led to our second-floor apartment, I saw a magnificent lobby as lovely as any in the finest hotel. When I actually entered our apartment, I was even more amazed. No longer were there the small rooms of my youth. Instead I beheld huge rooms, lavishly decorated. As

I walked from room to room, I discovered more beauty with each step. I could scarcely believe my eyes!

In the dream the Lord came to my side. I said to Him in wonder, "Jesus, it's all so transformed! Is this really the home where I grew up? How did it ever become this beautiful?" His answer to me came through a verse of Scripture. He said, "May you learn to value the things that really matter."

As I awoke, those words from Philippians 1:9-10 were emblazoned on my mind: "My prayer is that your love may more and more abound, both in understanding and wealth of experience, so that with a clear conscience and blameless conduct you may learn to value *the things that really matter, up to the very day of Christ.*"

Though in reality my home was rather modest, the Lord showed me through this dream what it looked like in His eyes. Despite our weaknesses and shortcomings as a family, we had a genuine concern and love for one another. That love gave our home a beauty and a value no property appraiser could estimate.

Devotion and sacrifice were a way of life for my parents as they cared for our needs. Our family spent time together doing things as simple as sharing a meal or taking a Sunday drive. Faithfulness and love were present in our home, and these reflections of the Lord's own presence accounted for the transformation in the dream.

In the midst of our society's growing materialism, you and I need to be reminded to value the things that really matter. It's not fine furniture, plush carpets, or the latest video equipment that will enrich our homes today. As Blessed Mother Teresa of Calcutta observes, those nations with the greatest material wealth are really the poorest of all. Why is this? She said it was because we have forgotten how to show the "understanding love" of Jesus to those in our families. We've closed our hearts to our own.

Blessed Mother Teresa prescribed a remedy that is simple but not easy. We need to begin to listen to each other, to try to understand each other, to forgive each other, and even to smile at each other. In short, we need to make peace with those in our families if we want the presence of Jesus to grace our homes.

And, it's never too late to begin again. It's never too late to learn to value the things that really matter. I recently heard of a couple who had been married for 43 years and who were having serious marital problems. After they committed themselves to pray daily for the grace to forgive each other, the peace of Jesus Christ began to transform their relationship. It's never too late to open our hearts to one another in love.

My prayer for your family and mine was contained in the Scripture verse from that memorable dream: *"May your love more and more abound—that you may learn to value the things that really matter, up to the very day of Christ."* (Philippians 1:10)

This I Know

Patrick's bedtime ritual is the same each night. First, a bath. Then jammies (pajamas). Prayers. A book followed by my medley of bedtime songs. Finally, a back rub. Sometimes we need to negotiate on the book. Patrick wants two long ones and I hold out for one short one. But we always agree on the medley.

I've crooned a different bedtime medley for each Mansfield child. For Patrick it's *Jesus Loves the Little Children, Immaculate Mary* (he joins in the Ave Maria) and that old standby, *Jesus Loves Me.* You remember this last song, don't you?

Jesus loves me, this I know
For the Bible tells me so.
Little ones to Him belong.
They are weak, but He is strong.
Yes, Jesus loves me,
Yes, Jesus loves me,
Yes, Jesus loves me,
The Bible tells me so.

When I sing the third verse, Patrick always perks up. In case you've never heard it, here it is:

Jesus loves me when I'm good,
When I do the things I should.
Jesus loves me when I'm bad,
Though it makes Him very sad.

"Why does Jesus love me when I'm bad, Mama?" Patrick asks with a twinkle in his eye. The idea of being naughty and getting away with it does have a certain appeal to a five-year-old! I try to explain that Jesus loves us all the time, even when we do bad things. In fact, there's nothing we can ever do to make Him stop loving us! He loves us when we obey Him, and He keeps loving us even when we disobey Him. He'll always love us, even when we wander far away from Him.

"But why does Jesus love me when I'm bad, Mom?" Patrick persists. "Because that's just the way He is, Sweetheart." Face-to-face with the mystery of God's love, my answer seems inadequate. It's not easy to explain unconditional love and mercy to a five-year-old. I just keep singing to him, "Jesus loves me. This I know," trusting that as Patrick grows up the miracle of God's merciful love will unfold in his life.

It's no wonder Patrick finds it hard to grasp the concept of God's unconditional love and commitment toward us. It defies human logic. God's actions are so unlike our own. For instance, when someone offends or disappoints us, we want to avoid that person. We withhold affection; we withdraw trust; we place conditions on our love. I'll love you if...I'll love you until...I'll love you unless...I'll love you except...

With Jesus, it's just the opposite. In His compassion, He reaches out all the more to the one who has offended Him. He's always ready to forgive and to forget, to welcome us back as intimate friends. In Isaiah we read, "Though your sins are like scarlet, they shall be white as snow" (Isaiah 1:18). And in Psalm 103:12, "As far as the east is from the west, so far does He remove our transgressions from us."

In fact, our very sins can be occasions of a deeper experience of God's love. St. Augustine knew this well after his conversion when he amended the famous passage from Romans 8:28: "God makes all things work together for good in the lives of those who love him..." "Even sin," added Augustine. The greater our need for mercy, the greater the mercy God supplies, for He is rich in mercy.

Let us ponder this amazing love and mercy of Jesus anew. His love for us does not depend on our goodness. Never has. Never will. Listen to St. Paul: "God shows His love for us in that while we were yet sinners, Christ died for us" (Romans 5:8).

Let's join in Patrick's childlike wonder at so great a love. Yes, "This I know, that God is for me" (Psalm 56:10). Jesus loves me and He loves you too—all the time—no matter what. It's just the way He is. God is love. How do I know? The Bible tells me so!

 Heirlooms

I have a confession to make. The bag I was clutching under my arm a moment ago is filled with fine fabric. The ad that read "50 to 70 percent off" sent me flying out the door to a fabric sale. Like most women who love to sew, I have a collection of fabric pieces that were just too reasonably-priced to pass up. Every so often I give some away, realizing that even if I live to the age of 100, I'll never complete all of the sewing projects I've created in my dreams.

It wasn't until my daughter's birth that I took an interest in heirloom quality clothing. Hand-smocked dresses are my special love because they're so delicate and feminine. After having had two boys who are only happy when clad in football jerseys, I longed for frills and lace on my little princess. Because the cost of fine clothing is so high, I decided to learn how to smock. So far I've made Marie-Thérèse several dozen dresses. This month she'll receive her First Communion wearing a dress I just completed. I hope this labor of love will become a family heirloom.

It's wonderful the way the Holy Spirit can use things from our everyday lives to teach us spiritual truth. Through my experience with heirloom sewing, He has helped me understand how God uses a sometimes painful process to prepare us for His purposes. This process bears similarities to the preparation I put my fabric through when creating an heirloom. From the fabric's point of view, it doesn't feel good!

The fabric must be laundered for shrinkage, torn, straightened, rolled tightly on a dowel, pierced with many needles to be pleated and finally blocked. All of this takes place before even one stitch of smocking is sewn.

Because of the precious time invested in making an heirloom, only the finest quality fabric is used. Anything less will not endure the test of time. If you're experiencing circumstances in your life that leave you feeling shrunk down to size, torn, and pierced, take heart! This is a sure sign you're being prepared for something special. Only quality fabric is treated this way!

The design on an heirloom garment is produced by a variety of smocking stitches, each one accomplishing something different. There are stitches that are hidden from view, but useful for stabilizing the entire work. Some stitches allow for stretching; others confine. There are stitches which appear uninteresting alone, but when stacked together, create wonderful pictures. The decorative stitches that attract the most attention are actually the least useful.

And so it is in our lives. The Divine Craftsman is creating a design of His own choosing, using the stitches that are needed at each moment. Sometimes we feel stretched, sometimes confined. At other times, a deep work of grace is taking place within us, but it's hidden from our sight. Frequently the Lord teaches us through a series of events that come together to form a picture He wants us to see. Only when completed can the full beauty of His work be appreciated, and that takes time.

A friend once told me, "Patti, these dresses are too time-consuming. Can't you sew a dress in less time?" My friend missed the point. I could quickly produce an acceptable garment, but not an heirloom. It brings me pleasure to make something beautiful and lasting. I want to create a one-of-a-kind heirloom, a labor of love, a work of art. God has that same desire in His dealings with us.

Scripture says, "We are God's work of art, created in Christ Jesus for good works which God prepared beforehand that we should walk in them" (Ephesians 2:10). God is preparing us in a painstaking manner through all of the experiences in our lives to be His work of art. Our Father is fashioning our character to be like that of Christ Jesus, His Son. And He has a work for us to do. Sometimes we'd rather not be made into heirlooms. We wish we could be sewn quickly.

I recently heard Mother Angelica's life story. She was abandoned by her father at the age of six. Poverty, loneliness, and despair were her constant companions. As a child she disliked school and people because of the rejection and pain they caused her. In addition to the interior suffering, Mother Angelica developed serious digestive problems and could find no cure. Finally, at the age of 18, she turned to God in prayer and was miraculously healed. Through this experience of God's love, she eventually discovered her vocation as a religious sister.

More suffering awaited her in the convent when a freak accident left her crippled. But through it all, God was fashioning Mother Angelica into a woman of great faith and love. He has used her in a remarkable way to found Eternal Word Television Network now broadcasting Catholic programs around the clock in the United States. Mother Angelica told us that God had to crush her through adversity to prepare her for His purposes.

God had a plan for her life, just as He has a plan for your life and mine. As we are prepared for the good works ahead, the process may be painful, but the Divine Craftsman knows precisely what He's doing. Don't doubt that for a minute. Trust Him. Yield to Him. He's making you into an heirloom, a work of art, that will serve His purposes and bring Him pleasure for all eternity.

The Sugar Bowl

There's an old-fashioned ice cream parlor in the town where my parents live. It's called The Sugar Bowl. This lovely place is replete with wrought iron chairs, round tables, pink striped wallpaper, pictures of ladies from long ago and more flavors of ice cream than you can imagine. It seemed to be the perfect spot to bring my daughter for a "girls day out."

At her suggestion, we invited Grandma to join us. After a delicious lunch we celebrated "just being together" with ice cream sundaes. Sitting at The Sugar Bowl restaurant with my daughter and mother, my heart rejoiced in the blessing of loving family relationships. But being at a restaurant called The Sugar Bowl reminded me of another sugar bowl from the past and the painful but necessary lesson the Lord taught me through it.

The summer after I was baptized in the Spirit I was scheduled to study in France. As a French major I wanted to perfect my accent and absorb French culture. But as much as I wanted to go to France, I sensed that the Lord was calling me to relinquish these travel plans in order to evangelize young people in the States. In fact, I found a desire growing within me to devote my life to full-time ministry rather than pursue a career teaching French.

This decision caused considerable anxiety in my parents. The Catholic Charismatic Renewal was still new, and it was difficult for them to understand the changes taking place in my life. In their love for me, they felt obliged to question my decision.

How well I remember the night my mother sat me down at the kitchen table to reason with me. Between us on the table was a sugar bowl which she used to illustrate her point. Mother said, "Suppose you are walking along a road and there is this obstacle in your path." She pointed to the sugar bowl. "Why not remove the obstacle temporarily and continue on the path you have already chosen?"

As I watched her move the sugar bowl back and forth across the table I thought, "That sugar bowl represents God and His will and purpose for my life. How can I postpone doing His will because it's different than what I planned?" I had a choice to make. Jesus says, "Whoever loves father and mother, son or daughter more than Me is not worthy of Me. He who will not take up his cross and come after Me is not worthy of Me" (Matthew 10:37-38). As much as I loved my mother and wanted to please her, I knew I could not push that sugar bowl aside. With real difficulty I explained my intention to do evangelistic work that summer and after graduation as well.

Although our relationship was strained for a while, my mother soon came to appreciate the grace of God in the Charismatic Renewal. In the years that followed, every member of my family was baptized in the Holy Spirit. God is faithful. He requires us to choose Him above any other relationship, any other love. But in doing so, He desires to shower His blessings on us and all those we love.

I thank God for sugar bowls—The Sugar Bowl Restaurant of recent times filled with the joy of celebration and the sugar bowl of long ago. It was the old sugar bowl on our kitchen table that taught me this: Choose God's will above all else. From that choice, blessings always flow into our lives and the lives of those we love.

The Eleventh Hour

"Pray for Jack. Pray for Jack." Every time my mother wrote or called, she made the same urgent request. Jack was dying of cancer and still had not turned to the Lord. His eternal destiny hung in the balance. Would he accept Jesus Christ as his Lord and Savior and enter into eternal life? Time was running out for Jack and he needed to make a decision. By our prayers we hoped to help him receive the grace of conversion.

Jack was married to my mother's friend, Peggy. Through their involvement in a prayer group, Peggy and Mom had become close sisters in the Lord, sharing each others joys and sorrows. Even before Jack was diagnosed with cancer, his salvation was of great concern to Peggy.

For many reasons they did not have a happy marriage. Although they enjoyed many of the Lord's blessings—a good job, nice home and healthy children—Jack would not acknowledge the Lord. His heart seemed closed to God.

As a young woman Peggy loved her husband. But over the course of time that love grew dim as he became more and more difficult to live with. At one point she seriously considered leaving him. But after she was baptized in the Holy Spirit, Peggy received the grace to persevere in her relationship with Jack despite the difficulties. The Lord helped her see that she was to be His instrument in Jack's life.

The one thing Peggy longed for was that her husband might come to know Jesus Christ and His love. After many years of prayer she saw little fruit. When Jack was diagnosed with cancer, her prayer became more fervent. While a physical healing would have been tremendous, the healing Jack needed even more was a spiritual one.

One day while preparing breakfast for Jack, Peggy realized that she should care for her husband as though she were caring for the needs of the Lord Himself. After that, she began to show Jack an even greater compassion and love, praying all the while that God's grace would touch him. Peggy was there for him during the dark days of his battle with cancer. It was the intercession of Mary, the mother of God, that helped Peggy receive the grace to say yes to the call to love Jack into eternal life.

As Jack's condition became more unstable, my mother asked me to join them in prayer. The doctor said Jack could slip into a coma anytime. He claimed to have no faith. He had never even been baptized and didn't want anyone to talk to him about God. One night, in desperation, Peggy cried out to the Lord, appealing to His mercy, and she felt in her heart there was a breakthrough. Her prayer had been answered.

Two days later, Jack called Peggy to his bedside and said he wanted to be baptized. He wanted to be a Catholic. When the priest came to see him, Jack said, "Father, I want you to know I'm not doing this just to please my wife. I'm doing it because I want to." You might say that was Jack's profession of faith. He had made his decision for Jesus Christ. It was their 32nd wedding anniversary!

Jack was baptized, anointed and received his First Holy Communion that day. God's love came alive in his heart because he was a new creation in Christ. He experienced the peace which surpasses understanding. My mom told me that he shed many tears of joy. Ten days later the Father called Jack home. He died, a man at peace with his God.

Like the laborers who were hired in the eleventh hour, he received a full day's pay as he entered into the joy of his Master.

The desire of Peggy's heart was granted. The years of perseverance in prayer and faithfulness in love were rewarded. "God wills that all men be saved and come to the knowledge of the truth" (I Timothy 2:4). He wanted Jack to know His saving love. He wanted Peggy to grow in holiness as she interceded for her husband.

Perhaps you have a husband, child or grandchild, a sister or brother, niece, nephew or friend for whose conversion you have been praying a long time. Jesus tells us to pray always and never lose heart. Every prayer is heard. "He wants none to perish, but all to come to repentance" (II Peter 3:9). Remember, Monica became a saint as she prayed 30 years for her son, Augustine. Persevere in prayer. Appeal to God's mercy. Be faithful in love. Whether sooner or later, God will honor your request. He may wait until the eleventh hour, but He is always sure to fulfill His word.

 Whispers

"If you lay your hands upon the young man seated next to you he will be healed," the Lord seemed to say. It was 1968 and the young man in question was a seminarian attending his first prayer meeting. During the course of the meeting, the Lord spoke to me interiorly in what I would call a gentle "whisper." I panicked!

"But, Lord, what if he isn't even sick? What if I scare him away? What if I'm dreaming this up? What if I pray and nothing happens? What if I wind up looking foolish? What if...What if...?"

I struggled through the next hour trying desperately to ignore the gentle whisper. After the meeting the seminarian turned to me and asked, "Is there someone here who can pray with me for healing? I'm wearing a back brace and came hoping to receive prayer." I felt relieved but ashamed. Indeed I had heard the Lord, but I lacked the faith to speak forth the word He had given me.

Through this experience the Lord taught me to have more confidence about those gentle "whispers" in the future. He encouraged me to act more quickly in obedience to His word. Had I yielded to the Spirit's promptings in this instance, the seminarian would have had a clear sign of God's personal concern. My reluctance hindered that expression of God's love for him.

"What I tell you in the dark, utter in the light; and what you hear whispered, proclaim upon the housetops," Jesus told His followers long ago (Matthew 10:27). His challenge is the same today. Yet, instead of speaking out boldly, we often cower in fear of what others may think of us if we proclaim God's word. Or we quench the Spirit because we're afraid of making a mistake.

It takes courage to yield to the spiritual gifts and to utter in the light what we've heard in the dark. Of course, all spiritual gifts must be tested and discerned, but they should not be stifled. Once we see how God's love breaks forth in the lives of others through the gifts of the Holy Spirit, we are encouraged to step out more in faith.

Recently I've come to a new appreciation of the beauty of the gift of revelation, sometimes called a word of knowledge. Here are a few examples from a recent conference of how powerfully God can manifest His personal love through this gift.

At a general session one of the speakers received this message: "Lorrie, the Lord has heard your prayers and will answer." A young woman told us later that she felt God touch her as that word was spoken. No one had called her by the nickname "Lorrie" since she was a child. Only someone who knew her intimately could address her in this endearing way. Lorrie and her husband had been praying earnestly for a baby to adopt. When she got home the night of the conference a surprise phone call confirmed that the adoption agency had started proceedings for the baby! That charismatic gift, that word of revelation, was a personal assurance from the Lord that He knew Lorrie by name, had heard her prayer and was blessing the adoption with this special sign of His love. Isn't God good?

Another word of revelation was given at that same conference concerning a woman who was dealing with a compromising situation and needed to repent. The speaker said, "Her name begins with the letter 'E.'" A woman who identified herself as "E" told us afterwards that she was being seduced by a married man at work. She came to the conference praying for the grace to break off the relationship. Her whole body became weak when this word of revelation was given, because she knew God was speaking to her directly. She realized she could not rationalize the situation any longer and repented. Hearing this word of revelation was the occasion of a deeper conversion in her life.

Many other words of revelation were proclaimed and confirmed at that conference, such as the healing of someone's right eye. A Christian counselor wrote us that he experienced an instantaneous healing of several floaters in his right eye. More importantly, he was able to approach his counseling with a renewed spiritual vision afterwards.

A young woman suffering from a knee injury heard a word of revelation proclaiming healing for a knee problem. Not only did she experience God's healing, but she even ran in the Crescent City Classic a few weeks later! Praise God!

How loving and gracious God is to show us His care through the gift of revelation. Let's pray for an even greater outpouring of such charismatic gifts in our midst, that all may come to know the power of the living God. Put aside fear and timidity when the Lord speaks. Be willing to be His instrument. What you hear in whispers, proclaim with faith and joy!

Jesus Put Them in Jail

"Mom, Patrick kept climbing in and out of my bed last night. He seemed really frightened about something."

This report from my daughter put me on the alert. Patrick, almost three years old at the time, must have had a bad dream. Later that day, when Patrick and I were alone, I decided to gently broach the subject.

"Honey, were you scared about something last night?", I inquired.

"Yes, Mom. Monsters coming to get me in bed. Me real scared." Patrick looked upset.

Like any concerned mother, I tried to allay his fears. At first, I took the tack that it was just a bad dream. Of course, there weren't *really* monsters in the room. I explained that nothing could hurt Patrick while he was in the safety of our home.

But Patrick didn't seem convinced. The monsters he saw were real enough to keep waking him up. "Me scared, Mom," Patrick insisted.

How does one explain a bad dream to a toddler? Then it dawned on me. Here was a truly "teachable moment," and I almost missed it. The Lord was presenting me with an opportunity to preach the good news to one of his littlest lambs.

"Patrick, do you know something? You don't ever have to be afraid of monsters again. The next time you have a bad dream just call on the name of Jesus. He'll come and make the monsters go away. Jesus is the Lord, and everything must obey Him."

Patrick's blue eyes opened wide, filled with trust in my word. "That's right," I assured him. "Just say 'Jesus' and He'll make the monsters go away." As I pronounced our Lord's name, I said it slowly and reverently. "Jesus."

"Jesus," Patrick repeated, just as slowly.

"Yes, call on Jesus, Patrick," I encouraged.

"Jesus...Jesus," Patrick replied.

Each time my baby pronounced the name of Jesus, it seemed to have greater unction. For several minutes the two of us drove along in our car, repeating the name of Jesus, echoing His blessed name to each other. It was a profound moment of grace.

As we invoked the glorious name of Jesus, that name above *all other names*, His own presence filled our car. Jesus Himself was there. "The Lord is near to all who call upon Him" (Psalm 145:18). Something happened to me, for sure. And I'm convinced that something happened to Patrick as well. Here's how I know.

About a week later Patrick awoke one morning and proudly announced, "Me have bad dreams again. Monsters scaring me. But me say 'Jesus, Jesus' and monsters go away. Jesus put them in jail!"

Alleluia! This was a real victory in a young life! The "putting them in jail" was Patrick's own idea, I'll have you know. In simple childlike terms Patrick was expressing a deep theological truth. Jesus saves and delivers His people! Satan has no hold on God's elect! In fact, in the words of St. John,

"The reason the Son of God appeared was to destroy the works of the devil" (I John 3:8). Fear, one of the devil's works, can be overcome by followers of Jesus.

And no child is too young to learn the power in the name of the Lord. I won't be with Patrick at every moment in his life when "monsters"—be they fears, worries, temptations, or difficulties—try to rob him of peace. But Jesus will! Jesus will! Teaching Patrick to call on the name of Jesus, and to experience His saving power, gives him the key to winning every spiritual battle in the future.

In the name of Jesus you too can find victory for your life. He is the Lord God of all flesh, and nothing is too difficult for Him. Trust in Him. Have confidence in Him. Call on His name. Teach your children, young and old, to invoke the all-powerful name of Jesus.

Yes, it's true. "The name of Lord is a strong tower. The just man runs to it and is safe" (Proverbs 18:10). "In the fear of the Lord is a strong defense. Even for one's children He will be a refuge" (Proverbs 14:26). Let's believe it!

Source of Death or Life

You've probably heard about the sermon that ran something like this. The preacher said, "We have to live holy lives!"

"Amen, brother," came the ready reply.

"We have to flee from sin!"

"Amen!"

"Avoid drinking and gambling!"

"Amen, brother!"

"We can't give in to sexual promiscuity."

"Amen. Amen."

"We can't repeat gossip."

Suddenly there was silence from the "Amen comer." One woman leaned to the next and said, "He was preaching before. Now he's gone to meddling!"

Isn't it interesting how readily we'll admit the need for self-control and discipline in other areas of our lives, yet refuse to acknowledge that the tongue must also he tamed? Consider these words of Jesus. "I tell you, on the day of judgment men will render account for every careless word they utter; for by your words you will be justified, and by your words you will be condemned" (Matthew 12:37). That passage makes me tremble!

Our eternal judgment is going to be based, to some extent, on what comes out of our mouths. How crucial it is that we learn to use our tongues rightly! "Death and life, good and evil, are in the power of the tongue" (Sirach 37:18). The ladies in the "Amen corner" wanted to deny the sinfulness of making critical, negative, unloving remarks. God has another opinion on the matter. He tells us to guard our speech.

The words of James 1:28 seem especially directed to people like us who want to grow in holiness. "If a man who does not control his tongue imagines that he is devout, he is self-deceived; his worship is pointless." Controlling our tongues is so central to our life with God that he warns us that if we don't bring this area of our behavior under control, the rest of what we do doesn't really matter. Did you ever stop to think about that?

Our words hold tremendous power over others. They can destroy or edify. One of the greatest ways we can express love is through our words, yet we tend to speak in the worst way to those we love the most. We say things to them we wouldn't dare say to others. For instance, one of my close friends from college was a beautiful person but she had a tendency to focus on the negative side of things. Until I was baptized in the Spirit, I didn't notice how critical her speech was. But eventually I came to realize how depressing it can be to listen to a constant string of negative remarks. I knew I needed to pray before, during and after conversations with her to keep a positive perspective. When I consciously interceded for her, there was usually an improvement in the tone of her speech.

Sometimes in the close circle of family and friends we can also indulge in negative humor. The rationalization that it's all in good fun just doesn't hold up. Ask the person who's been the object of negative humor. Take, for example, the husband at a dinner party who says, "If Shirley's cooking is as bad as usual, we'll send out for pizza," to which Shirley replies, "On your meager salary, we couldn't afford it!"

Everyone laughs, but the damage that's been done is anything but funny. My husband has drilled our children in this verse from Sirach 23:15, "A man who has the habit of abusive language will never mature in character as long as he lives." Abusive speech, even in a jesting manner hurts the hearer and the speaker as well.

On the other hand, the tongue can be a spring of living water. Years ago a woman from our prayer group underwent surgery. When I saw Camille's husband, I inquired about her health. "Even though she's in some pain," Don replied, "Camille has such a sweet and gentle way about her, she doesn't complain." I didn't know Camille very well at the time, but whenever I saw her in the future, Don's words were ringing in my ears. "Camille has such a sweet and gentle way about her, she doesn't complain." It was as if a tape recorder were playing in my mind to form an impression about Camille. What power Don held in that simple, loving description of his wife!

Let's renew our commitment to bring life, not death through our words with the help of the Holy Spirit. May the psalmist's prayer be our own. "Set a guard over my mouth, O Lord, keep watch over the door of my lips! Incline not my heart to any evil" (Psalm 141:3-4).

A Heart for God's People

Several months ago as I was seated at my sewing machine working on a dress for my daughter, my friend Jenny came to me. Well, let me explain. Jenny didn't exactly *come* to me, but the thought of Jenny was "gentle on my mind."

"Hum," I mused, "Haven't seen Jenny since her wedding last April. Wonder why I'm thinking of her? Maybe she needs prayer."

Without any special fanfare I simply commended her and all her needs to the Lord as I continued to sew. Soon afterwards I ran into Jenny's parents after Mass and inquired about her. Guess what? At the very time I felt prompted to pray for Jenny, she and her new husband David were trying to make an important decision concerning moving and work. It was a stressful situation for them. Jenny's parents were delighted to know I had been praying at that particular time. They took it as a sign of God's providence.

Just today I received a card from Jenny and David telling me how happy they are with their new home and work. Isn't God good to allow me to share in some small way in their need for prayer and their joy in being answered? I've often been the grateful recipient myself of such intercession. When someone is "gentle on your mind," it just might be a call to intercede.

"Intercession?" you say. "But isn't that something for monks or contemplative nuns?" Sure it is. But one of the wonderful works the Holy Spirit is doing today is to reawaken all God's people to a life of prayer. Yes, prayer—that means time spent alone seeking, loving, and adoring God. But it also means prayer *in the midst* of an active life. In fact, most of my intercession takes place while I'm working in the kitchen, laundry room, or driving in my car. Every day is filled with opportunities to intercede for God's mercy to break through. If you stay close to Jesus and open your heart to the Holy Spirit, you'll know when and how to pray.

For instance, my son turned on the World Series in October, 1989 and we were all suddenly riveted to the TV set watching the effects of the earthquake that devastated California. That's one time I knew I should pray. With my hand extended toward the image of people trapped in cars and buried under rubble, I interceded. No doubt, many did the same.

Once I was sitting with my family in a Pizza Hut, when a group of teenage boys dressed like punks passed by outside. That's another time I knew. "Instead of judging, pray," was the word that came to mind. Quietly I asked Jesus to reveal His love to each one of these boys. I unobtrusively sent a blessing their way with my lifted hand.

Sometimes prayer will lead to witnessing. Recently, the thought of a pharmacist at a nearby store kept "invading" my thoughts. I didn't even know his name, but the next time I was in the drugstore I told him that I'd been praying for him. He said that his wife was expecting a child so he appreciated the prayer. There was a brief opportunity to assure him of God's love. A few months later he eagerly showed me a photo of his healthy newborn son!

"The love of Christ *impels* us," wrote Saint Paul (II Corinthians 5:14). If God's love is in us, it must overflow to others. After my friend who is a nurse, committed her life to Christ she noticed a change in the way she cared for comatose patients.

In the past they seemed like little more than empty shells. Now, because she's alive with God's love, she prays for these precious souls while she works. What a glorious change!

Who are the people in your life, in your neighborhood, for whom the Lord wants you to intercede? The mailman? The boys who hang out on the corner? The woman on the news who lost a child? The co-worker with the unpleasant disposition? Ask the Lord to give you a heart for His people, and *you'll know.*

 # Behold the Cross

On June 10, 1990, I had a singular experience while praying before a magnificent life-size crucifix at the Church of St. Blase in Dubrovnik, Yugoslavia. After Mass we had a free afternoon to sightsee and shop in the beautiful old city. While I had every intention of strolling through Dubrovnik, I sensed a quiet interior call to remain behind in prayer. Then I discovered that beneath this exquisite portrayal of the crucified Lord is a reliquary containing a fragment of the true Cross which is venerated by a constant stream of pilgrims.

It is difficult to express what transpired in the time I knelt there, except to say that I experienced "the love of Christ which is beyond all knowledge." Hours sped by like moments as I beheld "the wood of the cross on which hung the salvation of the world." It was a sheer gift, all grace, totally undeserved—as every experience of God's love is. I felt myself irresistibly drawn, falling in love with His humanity, with His Passion.

He is indeed the Suffering Servant, meek and humble of heart. The wound in Jesus' side reminds us of the inexhaustible spring of mercy which flows from His heart toward those who take refuge there. The words of the *Anima Christi* echoed within me, "In Your wounds I fain would hide, ne'er to be parted from Your side."

I had some limited experience of what St. Paul meant when he wrote, "I have been crucified with Christ, and the life I live now is not my own; Christ is living in me" (Galatians 2:20). "May I never boast of anything but the cross of our Lord Jesus

Christ!" (Galatians 6:14). Behold the cross! Our salvation! Our healing! Our victory!

Later that day I met a woman from our group who asked if I had had a good afternoon. "Wonderful," I replied. "Look at this lovely necklace I bought," she said, "What did you buy?" How could I explain to her that I hadn't purchased anything money could buy? Rather, I had come to realize how Christ purchased me by the blood of His cross. I had discovered in a deeper way than before that Jesus Christ really is the pearl of great price, a treasure worth forfeiting everything else to possess. With renewed desire I was longing to "grasp the prize, since I have been grasped by Christ" (Philipians 3:12).

A friend of mine once told me that when she was troubled or lonely, she'd go sit quietly in church and look at the crucifix, just to remember what Jesus did for her. Somehow in light of His passion, her own burden seemed easier to bear. She knew that if Jesus loved her enough to lay down His life for her, He'd help her through whatever suffering she had to face. She had learned to behold the cross.

I've recently taken our own family crucifix down from the wall, dusted it off, and put it near the place I pray. Four-year-old Patrick keeps asking me, "Mama, why does Jesus have these big nails in His hands and His feet?" Why indeed? "Because He loves us, Patrick," I reply. Instinctively my son kisses the cross in gratitude for such love. Jesus is looking for companions of the cross, those who will return Him love for love.

One of the saddest verses to me in all of Scripture is from Luke 23:49. "All His friends were standing at a distance." While Jesus suffered on the cross very few dared to draw near. The *Imitation of Christ* speaks of the few lovers of the cross. How many would feast with Jesus and celebrate His miracles. Yet how few would fast with Him and bear humiliation for His sake.

Each Lent and every Friday the Church calls us to contemplate the mystery of the cross. I know the Holy Spirit wants to teach us how to love the cross in our daily lives. Here are just a few ideas. We can say "yes" to whatever God sends, stretching out our hands like Jesus, being nailed to God's will. That means we unite our joys and sorrows to Jesus' own sacrifice. Try giving thanks instead of grumbling. We can forgive "as soon as a quarrel begins", instead of waiting until the other guy apologizes first. We can serve the needs of others like Jesus who washed feet. Let's not be friends who stand at a distance from the cross.

I'm just a beginner in loving the cross, but perhaps this prayer of mine may help some of you. *"Lord Jesus, burn out of my heart a love for myself. Bum into my heart...a love for You and for Your cross. Amen."*

Her Favorite Child

Some of the best homilies I've heard were preached by a priest in campus ministry. He drew skillfully from his experiences of growing up in a large Irish Catholic family to both entertain and instruct us. We were captivated when he spoke because his stories always revealed something of God and the nature of His love.

Even now I vividly remember the story he told us about his mother. Having had nine children, she knew well the joys and challenges of motherhood. One day while she was ironing, a neighbor dropped in for a cup of tea. As usual, the conversation turned to the children.

"I don't know how you manage with such a large family and so many demands on you," commented her neighbor. Then lowering her voice the neighbor asked, "Come on, you can tell me. Which child is your favorite? There must be one who is easier than the rest. Surely there is one you love more than the others."

Listening from another room, the priest said he was anxious to hear his mother's answer. Certainly every child cherishes a secret hope that he or she is the favorite. At first his mother shook her head, refusing to answer. Then she protested that she had no favorites. She loved them all. But her friend was persistent. Finally she put down the iron and began her confession.

"Yes it's true. I do have a favorite. It's my oldest son looking for a job; he's my favorite. It's my daughter without a date for the prom; she's my favorite. And it's my son who's failing math; he's my favorite. It's my ten-year-old baseball player who didn't make the team; he's my favorite. It's my little one with the broken arm; she's my favorite. And on and on, his mother named each of her nine children with the particular reason why he or she was her favorite.

Instead of enumerating the talents and good qualities of each child, she spoke of their needs and suffering which called forth from her a special care and concern. With the tenderness and compassion of her mother's heart, she embraced each and every one of the nine as her "favorite child."

God's love for us is like that mother's love for her children. Should it surprise us that it's not our gifts, our talents or our successes that endear us to our God? But rather, it is our weakness, our need, our brokenness that makes each one of us His favorite. The more we need His mercy and His compassion, the more He gives Himself to us. With what confidence can we approach a God whose love for us is greater than that of any earthly parent.

St. Thérèse of Lisieux, the Little Flower, tells us that "the good God is more tender than a mother." And God's word assures that this is true. The Lord says, "Can a mother forget her infant; be without tenderness for the child of her womb? Even if she should forget, I will never forget you. See, upon the palms of my hands I have written your name" (Isaiah 49:15-16).

The Lord knows us. He loves us. He will never forget us. We are precious to Him. Our names are carved into the palms of His nail-pierced hands. He died and rose that we might live forever in heaven. That's really Good News!

Let's rejoice in the compassionate and tender love which mothers bear toward their children in need. Let's also rejoice in the source of that compassionate, tender love—the heart of God Himself!

Olympic Park

Do you remember being taught in catechism that at about age seven a child reaches the "age of reason"? This was the time when a youngster came to know the difference between right and wrong and to assume responsibility for his or her own actions.

I'm reminded of an experience I had when I was seven myself. This incident from my childhood stands out in vivid detail and has helped me over the years in my relationship with God the Father.

I'm sure that those of us who grew up in Irvington, New Jersey, were the envy of children everywhere. You see, on the outskirts of town was a huge amusement area called Olympic Park. This wonderful place was a child's delight, and I was especially fortunate because my dad took me there often.

What excitement I would feel as I got ready for a trip to Olympic Park! After paying admission you would pass through an area of mirrors that distorted your image in hilarious ways. As a little girl I loved to stand with my dad before one of the mirrors that made my six-foot tall father look short and stout. He was usually willing to pass from mirror to mirror so I could giggle to my heart's content.

The food at Olympic Park was scrumptious. There were things like hot dogs, ice cream and waffles, snowballs, and cotton candy. And the rides! It was impossible to take in everything on one visit. However, the ride we never missed was the giant carousel. This merry-go-round had beautiful hand-carved ponies and chariots that had come all the way from Germany. In fact, after Olympic Park closed, Disney World purchased the carousel, and it is still delighting children of all ages in Orlando, Florida.

Of course, I loved to ride the ponies and wave to my father as he watched me, but sometimes he would ride with me. We would sit together on a chariot, and I would pretend that he was king and I was his princess.

Besides all of that, there was a huge swimming pool, band concerts, and, best of all, a live circus. As you can tell, I loved Olympic Park not only because of all the delightful things to see and do, but because it was a special time to be with my father.

On one particular Saturday I was sure my dad was going to take me to the park. It was time for a new circus, the sun was shining, and I was ready to go. But my father had other plans. I really don't remember the reason we couldn't go, but I do remember my reaction. I was crushed. I had my heart set on going to the park, and I didn't like having my plans ruined. In typical little girl fashion, I pouted and fussed and fumed and cried. I tried every way I knew to convince my father to change his mind. Couldn't he see how miserable I was?

After some time, my father appeared in the doorway of my room and told me that he would bring me to Olympic Park after all. I'll never forget the experience of those next few moments. Instead of feeling happy that he had changed his mind, I felt a deep sadness. It was a moment of real grace in my young life. I realized that I could have my own way if I wanted it and that was a frightening discovery. Although my dad was willing to give in to me, it was clear that this was not his plan. My father would he there as always to provide for me and protect me at Olympic Park, but the joy would be missing.

Suddenly I came to see that there was a happiness I could only know when I was pleasing my father and doing his will, not my own. As we left for the park, one little seven-year-old girl felt a deep disappointment in herself and resolved to try not to act that way again. I was beginning to grow up.

Jesus said, "I always do what pleases my Father" (John 8:29) and "My meat and drink is to do the Father's will" (John 4:34). Pleasing the Father, doing the Father's will was the delight of Jesus. It is also the delight of every true follower of the Lord. In His will is our peace and happiness. Our Heavenly Father does not stop loving us when we fuss and fume and pout, trying to have our own ways. But by pleasing ourselves first, we are cut off from His joy.

Let's pray that we will reach and remain at the "age of reason." May our delight be more and more to please our Father in heaven and to do His will at all times.

And All Your Household

"It's all your fault for sending her to a Catholic school!"

"Don't tell me she's going to be a nun!"

"Why does Patti's roommate think she's crazy?"

These were some of the comments exchanged by members of my family after that famous phone call during which I told them about the Baptism in the Holy Spirit. In 1967, there were no books Mom and Dad could read, no teachings to listen to, no Papal statements to assure them that their daughter was still sane.

I'm afraid I did very little to quell their fears as I described the tingling sensation in my hands, praying in unknown tongues, and being knocked over by the power of God while kneeling before the Blessed Sacrament. No wonder my family was lamenting the fact that this strange thing had to happen to one of their own!

Overnight, it seemed, I had become a different person. My interests, ambitions, speech, dress and friendships changed. I had undergone a conversion experience and it touched every aspect of my life. Not all the changes were good. For example, I tended to isolate myself from family members and activities. Unwittingly, I was making it more difficult for them to respond in a positive way to my new walk with the Lord. Only as I matured in the Spirit, did I learn how to witness to them with greater sensitivity. The desire of my heart was to share with my family the joy and peace I'd found in surrendering my life to Jesus.

As I sought the Lord for wisdom, two inspirations came which proved to be very fruitful.

The first inspiration was to pray in a consistent, determined way for them. In 1968, I heard Ralph Martin share that he had set aside one day a week to intercede for his family. Encouraged by his example, I too began to pray and sacrifice every Thursday for my family, interceding that each of them might come to know the Lord in a personal way.

The second inspiration came as I was making a visit to the parish of my youth, Immaculate Heart of Mary Church in Maplewood, New Jersey. There in an alcove is a life-sized wooden statue of Mary seated with the Infant Jesus on her lap. She looks womanly yet strong, worthy of trust, able to care for all those entrusted to her. As I knelt at the altar I felt inspired to entrust every member of my family to Mary. As I did, a deep peace came over me.

I love to think of Mary before the throne of her Son in constant intercession for the needs of all God's children. So often I feel my own prayer is limited because of distractions and lack of confidence. But Mary is not distracted. She doesn't grow weary and she doesn't forget. Her entire being has been yielded to proclaim the greatness of the Lord and to bring others to Him. As we entrust our lives and loved ones to Mary, she takes responsibility for us as she speaks to her Son. "They have no more wine," Mary said at Cana. In response to her words, Jesus performed a miracle there. He continues to honor her requests today.

So I prayed and Mary prayed. Within one year, my two sisters and my mother were baptized in the Holy Spirit. I'll never forget the day my mother told me she wanted to be baptized in the Spirit. I was so thrilled I didn't know what to do or say! "Wait here, Mom, I'll get someone to talk to you," I blurted.

Five years passed. I continued to pray and sacrifice on Thursdays and entrust my family to Mary. As May, 1973, approached, I felt led to ask my mother and sisters to join me in praying for my dad. During the month of May we agreed to pray the rosary daily for him. On May 4th a relative invited my dad to make a Life in the Spirit Seminar. Wonder of wonders, Dad agreed! We had invited Dad to a Seminar many times before and he had always refused. By God's providence, I was home in New Jersey the night he was prayed with for the Baptism in the Spirit. Dad later told us he smelled the distinct aroma of incense—a beautiful sign of the presence of God.

From my immediate family, only my brother was not yet baptized in the Spirit. Nine years passed. We continued to pray. In February, 1982, while my brother was jogging, the Lord Jesus appeared to him on the road with arms outstretched. "Come to Me, Peter," Jesus beckoned. Peter said that as he began running toward Jesus, the vision faded but he continued to hear the Lord's voice. There on the road he surrendered his life to Jesus and was filled with the Holy Spirit. Imagine my joy when he called with the news! I was especially touched when I realized his encounter with the Lord took place on a Thursday (my regular day to intercede for my family), the Feast of Our Lady of Lourdes. No coincidence I'm sure. A week later he was prayed for with the laying on of hands. This was the 15th anniversary of my own Baptism in the Spirit. What a wonderful anniversary gift! How faithful our God is!

Remember the jailer in the Acts of the Apostles who asked what he must do to be saved? "Believe in the Lord Jesus and you will be saved, and all your household" (Acts 16:31). When this one man came to the Lord, so did his entire family. I believe we can hope and pray for the same grace in our own lives.

Perpetual Pentecost

A few months ago I was attending Mass at a college seminary nearby. As I watched the young seminarians receive Communion I began to pray that they might be filled with the Holy Spirit. "Lord," I prayed, "please show me what more I can do to help men like these receive the Baptism in the Spirit. I believe this grace is meant for the whole Church." Immediately after Mass one of the seminarians invited Al and me to come back in a few weeks to speak to them about the Charismatic Renewal. What a quick answer to prayer! I was thrilled.

As we considered what to tell these seminarians about the modern-day movement of the Spirit, we decided to start with Blessed Elena Guerra. Have you ever heard of her? Until recently I didn't realize how deeply indebted we all are to this remarkable Italian nun who lived at the turn of the last century. This is what we told our young seminary friends.

The Lord revealed to Elena Guerra the importance of continually invoking the Holy Spirit. He gave her a holy boldness to write twelve letters to Pope Leo XIII urging him to renew the Church by fostering a greater devotion to the Holy Spirit. Sensing God's voice speaking through Sr. Elena, the Holy Father asked all the bishops to conduct a solemn novena to the Spirit prior to Pentecost. He wanted this novena held annually, so that the Church might become a "praying Cenacle."

To further emphasize his point, Pope Leo XIII wrote an encyclical on the Holy Spirit. At Sr. Elena's suggestion, in the first moments of January 1, 1901, he dedicated the 20th century to the Holy Spirit and solemnly chanted the *Veni Creator Spiritus* (Come Creator Spirit) in the name of the whole Church. His action, prompted by Sr. Elena, was prophetic, for indeed this century has been marked by a sovereign outpouring of the Spirit of God.

At the time, however, Sr. Elena was deeply disappointed that there was such a poor response among Catholics to the Pope's plea for prayer to the Spirit. Unbeknownst to her, on the evening of December 31, 1900 another group of Christians were ready and willing to seek more of the Holy Spirit in their lives. In Topeka, Kansas, a young woman named Agnes Ozman asked Reverend Charles Parham to pray for her to be baptized in the Holy Spirit. This occasion is generally accepted as the beginning of the pentecostal movement. It was only years later that Catholics in large numbers began to experience the grace of the Baptism in the Spirit. Interestingly enough, on that very site in Topeka, Kansas there now stands a Catholic Church, Most Pure Heart of Mary, where a Catholic Charismatic prayer group met!

More than half a century after Elena Guerra's inspiration, Pope Saint John XXIII echoed her desire for more of the Holy Spirit when he had the entire Church pray for the success of the Vatican Council. "Renew your wonders in this our day as by a new Pentecost."

The sovereign outpouring of the Spirit that began in 1967 among Catholics in the Charismatic Renewal was an answer to the prayer called for by Sr. Elena Guerra in the beginning of this century. Thank you, Blessed Elena Guerra, for helping us to experience this new Pentecost!

After sharing these things with the seminarians, we gave testimony about how the Baptism in the Spirit has helped us love Jesus and the Church more deeply. We know that the release of the power of the Holy Spirit and His gifts is meant for everyone in the Church. God desires to give far more than we desire to receive.

After we spoke, almost every one of the seminarians came forward to receive prayer for more of the Holy Spirit in his life. Surely these young men will need an ongoing Pentecost to be effective priests. What joy to see their hunger for God!

Not only on the great feast of Pentecost, but every day let us cry out to the whole Church with Blessed Elena Guerra:

> *Pentecost is not over. In fact, it is continually going on in every time and in every place, because the Holy Spirit desired to give Himself to all men and all who want Him can always receive Him, so we do not have to envy the apostles and the first believers; we only have to dispose ourselves like them to receive Him well, and He will come to us as he did to them... It is necessary that we return to the Holy Spirit so that the Holy Spirit may return to us.*

Together, brothers and sisters, may we become a *praying cenacle*—always expecting, always receiving, a *perpetual Pentecost!*

At Your Altars

I am a mother...and this "being a mother" is part of my life of prayer. Any mother worthy of the name cares about her children whether they are young or old. Whenever I come before the Lord in prayer, I take my children with me—their needs, their sufferings, their desires. But I have found that it's all too easy to pray for my children without really surrendering them to the Lord. It's not enough to be concerned about their welfare; we must really trust that the Lord cares for them more than we do and that He will help them. The Holy Spirit, the greatest teacher, will teach us how to pray and to trust God for our families if we allow the word of God to form us.

One day, not too long ago, I was very burdened about one of our children. A priest who is a dear friend reminded me of this verse from the Bible, "Cast all your cares on Him, for He cares for you" (I Peter 5:7). In the light of this Bible verse, I could see that although I'd pray for my child, I would still worry—feeling like it was I who was still carrying the burden. Then later in the day I was reminded of a verse from one of the psalms: "Grace and glory He bestows, no good thing does the Lord withhold from him who walks uprightly." When I had a chance to pray in church about the situation with my child, I found a place up as close as possible to the Blessed Sacrament altar. I searched for the psalm which has been on my mind and discovered that it is Psalm 84. Perhaps you may remember some of its verses. "How lovely is Your dwelling place, O Lord of Hosts. My soul yearns, yea pines, for the courts of the Lord. Even the sparrow finds a home, and the swallow a nest in which to lay her young, at Your altars, O Lord of Hosts, my King and my God!"

Here it was—just the image I needed to help me surrender my child! These verses inspired and then formed my prayer as I began to speak to the Lord so close to His altar. "Jesus, even the sparrow finds a home in which to lay her young at Your altar. You tell me in Your word that I am worth more than many sparrows. So surely, here at Your altar, there is a place for my young—for each of my children. For what is mine is Yours and what is Yours is mine. If you withhold no good thing from those who walk in sincerity, then I should have nothing to fear. For You will not fail to give my children all that they truly need for their growth—every good thing, especially the consolation of Your Holy Spirit, the greatest of all good gifts." Consciously I then laid at His altar each of my children, especially the one for whom I had the greatest concern. I left the church unburdened and within a short time some wonderful things took place in my son's life—signs of the Lord's care for his deepest needs.

The Bible can teach us as parents how to pray with confidence and trust. Another verse which has been forming my prayer for my family these days has been this one: "Here I am with the children God has given me." (Hebrews 2:13). It's true that in some way we must come to God alone—that God has no grandchildren—each person must come to a mature commitment of his or her life to God. And yet, it is also true that we never really come to Him alone—especially if we are parents. I am always before God as mother of Mark, Peter, Marie-Thérèse and Patrick. And even when this prayer is unspoken, it is nevertheless in my heart, "Here I am with the children God has given me." They are mine, but they are only lent to me by the Lord. Ultimately they are His. And it is with this realization that I must pray. God knew them before they were formed in my womb. He called them each by name before I ever pronounced their names. This thought fills me with confidence, knowing that I am not trying to convince the Lord to do something good for my children as though I am the only one who knows, understands and loves them. He does, and far better than I!

After my own mother was called home to heaven I have been consoled by this thought in the midst of my sadness at losing her earthly presence. A mother takes with her into eternity her love for each of her children, her intimate knowledge of each one. As an intercessor, with a more intense gaze upon the Lord, she can speak to Him about the needs of her children. What confidence the vision of God must give to such prayer! If here on earth our confidence grows as we feed on the word of God in the Scripture and in the Eucharist, how much greater and stronger our confidence will become when we no longer see "in a mirror dimly," but rather "face to face!" (cf. I Corinthians 13:12).

O Glorious St. Joseph

In addition to the feast of St. Joseph celebrated on March 19, you probably know that May 1 is the Feast of St. Joseph the Worker, the just man, husband to Mary, foster father of Jesus, hailed by Popes as the protector of the universal Church. I knew all those facts from childhood too. But what I didn't know until recently was the tremendous power St. Joseph has to intercede for us. Even living in New Orleans, Louisiana where Italian-Americans hold St. Joseph in great honor, even witnessing the deep devotion to St. Joseph of my father-in-law and husband, even after naming our first child Mark Joseph, I still had no relationship with the glorious saint myself.

Sure, there was the time years ago when I needed a job and my friend, who had been a Sister of St. Joseph, began to invoke his help. Within days we were both hired as religion teachers at a prestigious high school. Then there was the time we were selling our family car and my husband put the sale in St. Joseph's hands. The first day the newspaper ad ran, the first person who called, offered us the exact amount we were asking in cash! Yet, those were answers to other people's prayer, not my own.

Then, in July, 1989, as I stood before a beautiful statue of St. Joseph cradling the child Jesus, something happened. A bond was established. It was simply a grace. In the ensuing months, I found myself confiding my father's health to St. Joseph's care. Before the end of that year, my dad was rushed to the hospital for emergency bypass surgery. It was a close call, but my dad came through, thanks to the prayer of St. Joseph! Joseph had gotten my attention.

About that time our family began a novena to St. Joseph because of a special financial need. On the eighth day of the novena our son, Peter, asked, "Is the money coming tomorrow, Dad?" Now that's faith! We explained that we weren't sure how or when the answer would come, but we knew that it would come. Within a few weeks we had a dramatic answer to our financial need from an anonymous source. St. Joseph had me won over completely. Forever will I sing his praises.

Soon afterwards as I was reading the autobiography of St. Teresa of Avila, I learned of her tremendous devotion to St. Joseph. Teresa, a Doctor of the Church, speaks convincingly about the power of Joseph's intercession. Listen to her own words:

> *I took as my advocate and Lord the glorious St. Joseph and earnestly recommended myself to him. I saw clearly that as in this need, so in other greater ones, this father and lord of mine came to my rescue in better ways than I knew how to ask for. I do not recall up to this day ever having petitioned him for anything that he failed to grant. It is an amazing thing the great and many favors God has granted me through the mediation of this blessed saint, the dangers I was freed from both of body and soul. The Lord wants us to understand that just as He was subject to St. Joseph on earth—for since bearing the title of father, being the Lord's tutor, Joseph could give the Child commands— so in heaven. God does whatever Joseph commands.*

What a marvelous insight! In heaven, Jesus continues to listen attentively to the requests of his foster father, Joseph. Joseph has special influence with his beloved Son. Of course, we know that we can approach God directly with our needs and He hears and answers us in love. Yet, for His own mysterious purpose, God chooses to be glorified in His saints. He delights to send us His blessing as we invoke the help of one who has served Him so well in this life—one like the glorious St. Joseph.

So, St. Teresa says, "Try it and you'll see!" Go to Joseph. Like Mary did. Like Jesus did. I am convinced that God is calling us today to rediscover St. Joseph's power, and I'm in good company. Read the Pope Saint John Paul II's Apostolic Exhortation about St. Joseph entitled *Guardian of the Redeemer*. After expounding on Joseph's life, the Pope expresses his desire that "the whole Christian people not only will turn to St. Joseph with greater fervor and invoke his patronage with trust, but also will keep before their eyes his humble, mature way of serving and of 'taking part' in the plan of salvation."

Having experienced for myself the power of St. Joseph, I am determined to place everything in my life under his patronage. I want his hand on me, even as it was on Jesus: training, guiding, providing, protecting. I'm asking him to teach me to pray. He lived his whole life in the company of Jesus and Mary, speaking to them, listening to them, serving them. St. Teresa tells us that Joseph is a tremendous help to anyone serious about prayer and holiness of life.

May we recall the words spoken long ago to God's people when they were seeking provision in their lives. *"Ite ad Joseph! Go to Joseph!"*

The Beauty Parlor

You know how you feel when you're overdue for a haircut? Well, I felt that way for several weeks before I was able to get to the beauty parlor. I hated to take the last appointment on a Friday evening, but it was the only time available.

The owner of the shop was on hand that evening to make suggestions to some newly trained beauticians concerning each customer. A simple haircut was all I wanted, but when my turn came, the owner had something else in mind. He turned my head from side to side in dismay. "You certainly need to do something with this hair," he insisted. "It will never do to keep wearing it like this."

Then he told the beautician exactly how to cut my hair, what kind of special conditioner I needed, and which permanent wave to give me. When I explained that I wasn't planning on getting a perm, he told me that I needed to "get more involved with my hair" if I wanted it to look good.

This whole exchange took place in the presence of several other customers. Far from feeling grateful for the special attention, I was utterly humiliated. By the time he finished his "beauty" analysis, I felt positively ugly. I could afford neither the time nor the expense involved in getting a perm that night, and I was embarrassed to have to make a public explanation.

As the beautician washed my hair, I closed my eyes and began to speak to the Lord in my heart. The humiliation and embarrassment I had just experienced made me realize my need for Him and His consolation. I was content to be still and draw near to Jesus in prayer as my haircut began, but the beautician, Marcia, wanted to talk.

I had never met her before but Marcia shared freely about her husband and young daughter. Even though I wasn't offering much information about my life, she seemed very interested in me. In response to her question about my field of work, I told her that I used to work in campus ministry. She prodded me to describe what I did. In very general terms I explained that I tried to help the students draw closer to God. At the mention of the Lord's name, Marcia stopped cutting my hair and looked at me in the mirror. "Oh please," she pleaded, "tell me whatever you used to tell those students. I so much want to know God better. If fact, I just asked my husband to buy me a Bible. *Please, please, tell me about God."*

By this time the salon was empty except for the two of us. As Marcia continued to cut my hair, I had complete freedom to speak to her of God's love. Her questions were earnest and beautiful. She wanted to know how to repent, how to confess her sins, how to pray, how to teach her child about the Lord. We talked for a long time about her relationship with Jesus.

Before leaving, I showed her how to pray with her child and make a small sign of the cross on her forehead in blessing. It was my way of laying hands on Marcia to bless her at the end of our wonderful sharing.

Marcia marveled at our "chance" meeting. It was her last day at this particular beauty shop and I was her last appointment! But you and I know this meeting was hardly by chance. The Lord had prepared her heart for our encounter by creating in her a hunger for Himself. And the Lord had prepared my heart by allowing me to experience a humiliation that helped me seek His presence.

Do you know what? As I left the beauty parlor that night, I really did feel beautiful! But it wasn't because of a special conditioner or permanent wave. In His mercy God had opened a door for me to share His love with someone in need and clothed in that love we were both made beautiful.

What About Me?

Does this sound familiar? For weeks you've planned a special birthday party for one of your children. Invitations have been mailed out. Party plates, cups, hats, and favors have all been purchased. You may have even tried your hand at decorating a cartoon character cake. You've decided how many games will be needed to keep the children occupied. Gifts have been wrapped and the house is all decorated with balloons and streamers. Finally everything's ready for a celebration which should be a happy occasion for the whole family.

But what's that sound? Who could it be crying in the bedroom? Upon investigation you find one of your younger children sobbing dejectedly. The cause? You guessed it—his brother's birthday party.

It's difficult for this little one to understand why Mom is giving so much time and attention to the birthday child. He doesn't remember that you've done exactly the same thing on his birthday. All he knows is that right now someone else is in the limelight. Feelings of jealousy, competition, and insecurity surface. Then come the inevitable questions: "But, what about me, Mom? Don't you care about me? When's my turn? What about me?"

I suppose that anyone who has more than one child is familiar with this question. Each sibling seems to need constant reassurance that he or she is special, unique, and cherished. And the question, "What about me?" doesn't end with childhood either. Even adults ask it. I was reminded of this recently while listening to my daughter read to me out loud the gospel story of two grown sisters who were friends of Jesus—Martha and Mary.

Hearing the familiar passage from Luke 10 as it was paraphrased in children's language, the story took on fresh meaning. I could picture Jesus at the home of Martha and Mary. The Lord had a deep love for each of these women. He wanted each of them to know the joy of His presence. Mary responded immediately by looking at Jesus and listening to Him. Her heart was undivided. She was given wholly to the Lord. Martha on the other hand, was "anxious and upset about many things" (Luke 10:41). She too loved Jesus and was happy to have Him present, but she was distracted.

Could be that it was not only the "details of hospitality" that occupied and upset her? Perhaps poor Martha was also troubled that her sister Mary seemed to be getting all the attention. Just think of what Martha said to Jesus, *"Lord, are you not concerned* that my sister has left me to do the household tasks all alone? Tell her to help me" (Luke 10:40). *"Don't you care, Lord?",* another translation reads. Martha's unspoken question to Jesus was that familiar query, *"What about me?"*

When my daughter finished reading the story, we discussed it together. As we talked, she made the following observation: "If Martha wasn't grumbling and complaining so much about her sister, she could have done her work and listened to Jesus at the same time!" My little girl had a real insight.

I don't think it was just the housework that kept Martha from experiencing peace and joy in Jesus' presence. There was something else bothering her. She was upset with Mary who was sitting at Jesus' feet. Martha was afraid that her sister was receiving more from Jesus than she was. In short, she felt left out. The Lord didn't chide Martha because she was preparing a meal for him. Rather, there was something in her attitude that needed correction before she could perceive His special love for her.

Aren't we sometimes the same way? Either we're busy grumbling about our own circumstances or envying someone else's. Because of our self-centered attitude, we miss the fact that Jesus is present, loving us and trying to speak to us.

In answer to the question, "What about me?" the Lord may want to reassure us in the same way I've reassured each of my children. He would say, *"Don't be jealous of your brother or sister. You're special to Me too. No one can ever take your place in My heart. I may have given someone else a gift you like, but I've chosen a gift for you as well. Be at peace and rest assured that I really love you."*

Disdain Not

"Shh! stand over there so she doesn't see!" said my son, Peter, in a loud whisper.

"Put it on the bottom shelf," replied my daughter.

Our family had stopped into a Christian bookstore and we were scattered in different directions browsing through the gift items. I couldn't imagine what my two children were up to. Perhaps they'd broken something and were hiding the evidence. As I went to investigate, my little culprits got quickly to their feet. It was obvious they were trying to hide something by the looks of guilt on their faces.

"Okay, move over," I said, prepared for the worst. I knew the rule, "If your children break it, it's yours." Instead of a shattered mug, I found a long wooden paddle with the words inscribed, "Withhold not correction from your child" (Proverbs 23:13).

Once my two little ones spied that paddle they panicked. This was one gift item they definitely did not want!

"Really, Mom, don't get this paddle," they protested. "We don't need it!"

When we were first married, my husband did a Scripture study on child rearing. It was impressive to read the list of Bible passages he assembled concerning children. What's clear from the Bible is that discipline and training play a great part in raising our children. Of course, we need to show them affection, care, and concern, but we must also he vigilant about correcting them if we really love them. Parents have the awesome responsibility of raising their children in the ways of God and this takes not only love and wisdom, but also discipline.

I could appreciate these truths from a parent's point of view quite easily. Then one day it occurred to me that I was God's child. As my heavenly Father, He applies these same principles in disciplining me. What a sobering thought!

I've become very familiar with the passage from Hebrews 12 concerning the discipline of the Lord. Early in our married life a brother in Christ with a special gift of revelation visited our prayer group. With amazing accuracy, he gave each person a Scripture passage pertinent to his or her life even though he had never met any of us before. Most passages were to console, upbuild and exhort. I couldn't wait to hear his word for us. When our turn finally came, he gave us a word which we still have in our Bible today. "For the moment all discipline seems painful rather than pleasant; later it yields the peaceful fruit of righteousness to those who have been trained by it" (Hebrews 12:11). Can I admit to you I was disappointed? Of all the great and glorious promises we could have received, the one God chose for us was a promise of discipline. Ouch! I too felt like hiding the paddle.

The writer of Hebrews is fully sympathetic with our human response to discipline. *We don't like it.* That's why he reminds us of a verse found in Proverbs 3:11-12. "Disdain not the discipline of the Lord nor lose heart when He reproves you. For whom the Lord loves, He disciplines; He scourges every son He receives." *Disdain not His discipline. Disdain not His correction.* Our Father in heaven is more loving and wise than any earthly parent, and whatever discipline He allows is for our good. Of course, it takes a certain maturity to recognize His love when discipline comes.

Can you picture the typical scene of a parent and little child when correction has to take place? The child cries, "You don't love me anymore, if you loved me you wouldn't punish me." The parents' reply? "No, it's because I love you that I have to correct you."

So often in our response to discipline we are like little children. We conclude that God doesn't love us; we cry and pout. But the Scripture reassures us, "Whom the Lord *loves*, He disciplines..." And why? God disciplines us because he wants us to share His very own holiness. He's preparing us for an eternity of glory with Him.

Let's remember we have a Father in heaven who loves us. "We have had earthly fathers to discipline us and we respected them. Shall we not much more be subject to the Father of spirits and live?" (Hebrews 12:9). Instead of grumbling and complaining the next time we're corrected, let's see it as a sign of our heavenly Father's love. Let's resolve to disdain not the discipline of the Lord.

 # Be Prepared

I've never been a "morning person", even though I know great blessings are reserved for those who seek God in the early morning hours. Unfortunately, I'm rarely alert enough then to pray very well. Perhaps this is why I wasn't prepared the morning I met Ross at the airport.

Because I had to catch an early plane, I left home without breakfast. At the airport snack bar I ordered a cup of tea. Next to me stood a man in his thirties who was dressed like a teenager. He had long blond hair, jeans and a matching jacket.

"Good morning," he said, smiling in my direction. "This waitress mixes a spicy Bloody Mary if you're interested. Give me another one, Honey, but hold the tabasco." Leaning toward me he added, "The spirit is willing but the flesh is weak."

What's with this guy, I wondered? Is he flirting? Drunk? Lonely? Or could it be that the Lord wants me to witness to him? To be perfectly honest, I wasn't prepared. All I wanted was a cup of tea to help me wake up. I wasn't sure how to begin evangelizing him, but he took the initiative himself.

"My name is Ross. I'm on my way to Las Vegas to gamble. Who are you and where are you headed?"

Still reluctant, I gave a minimum of information. "I'm speaking at a conference in Lake Charles."

"Really, what are you speaking about?" (Most people don't want to know.)

"I'm speaking about Mary, the Mother of God." I sipped my tea, sure my answer would draw our conversation to a rapid conclusion.

"Mary, huh? What are you saying about Mary?"

I pushed my tea aside, and with a silent "Come, Holy Spirit" began to share how God chose Mary in His plan to bring forth Jesus, the Savior of the world. The purpose of her life was to give us Jesus, and even today she is leading people to God.

I asked if he had heard of the apparitions of Our Lady and he had. "Well, Ross, when Mary has appeared in places like Lourdes and Fatima, she's come to young people with a simple but urgent message. She's calling for faith in God, conversion to Christ, prayer, fasting and peace."

By now he was clearly uncomfortable. Ross had already told me he was thirty but still wondering what to do "when he grew up."

He was unemployed yet planning to gamble what little money he had in Vegas. His life was without purpose. "Peace, humph! World peace is impossible!" he retorted.

With only a few minutes left, I knew I had to challenge Ross clearly and directly to commit his life to Christ. I said, "Let's bring peace closer to home. Mary is inviting each one of us to give our lives to God, so peace can begin in our hearts. Have you ever given your life to God, Ross?"

"Yeah, but I don't think He wants my life," Ross responded sullenly.

My flight was now boarding. "Look Ross, I know God wants your life. He wants every life. You need to discover His will, but that can only happen by complete surrender, no strings attached. Pray. Give your life to God. Ask for His guidance, and He'll answer you," I assured him.

"How can you be so sure?" Ross asked.

My answer was simple. "I know Him."

As I left Ross stirring his drink, he looked considerably less cheerful than before. How I wished I could have done more to help him. If I were better prepared, I would have had a prayer card or booklet ready to give him, or I could have offered to pray with him. But despite my sleepiness and reluctance, God used me to speak a word of truth to Ross before he left for Las Vegas.

At the conference I asked people to pray for Ross, that the Hound of Heaven would pursue him until he gives his life completely to God. Will you please pray for him too?

I'm convinced there are millions like Ross searching for God even as they run from this Hound of Heaven "down the nights and down the days...down the arches of the years...down the labyrinthine ways." We are the ones God wants to use to call them to Himself. So, at all times "*be prepared* to give reason for the hope that is in you" (I Peter 3:15).

Why I Love the Holy Spirit

When our second son, Peter, was about to be confirmed, I wrote him a letter I entitled, "Why I Love the Holy Spirit." Here it is:

Dear Peter,

How well I remember my own preparation for Confirmation. We sang, "Come Holy Ghost," memorized catechism, pondered Confirmation names, and worried about how hard the bishop might slap us! I was excited about the jewelry I'd receive as a Confirmation gift.

We didn't have religious sisters in our parish, so a different nun would be on hand each day after school to instruct us. Was it ever confusing! One day Sr. Rita warned us not to embarrass her by giving the bishop the wrong answer to any questions. Then in comes Sr. Clare saying that she wanted us to make a good showing, and that everyone should raise his hand, with or without the right answer!

All in all, Peter, the Holy Spirit was still a mysterious "Ghost" for me at the age of 12. I could relate to God the Father because I knew how kind and loving Grandpa Gallagher was to me. I knew Jesus through the Gospels. But when it came to the Holy Spirit, I drew a blank.

Then about eight years later, a wonderful thing

happened to me on a retreat that later became known as the Duquesne Weekend. I decided to surrender my whole life to God. Once I agreed to let Jesus have His way in my life and invited the Holy Spirit to act, everything changed. No longer was the Holy Spirit a faraway heavenly dove. I began to experience the Spirit as a Person, who was very present, helping me to know and love Jesus, teaching me to proclaim that Jesus is Lord.

St. Paul says, "The love of God has been poured into our hearts by the Holy Spirit," and it's really true, Peter. As you receive the Holy Spirit in Confirmation you'll be able to love God more than before because it will be the Holy Spirit living in and through you That's why He's called the "sweet guest of the soul." He actually makes His home in us!

As much as Dad and I love you, we can't always be present, nor can we give you advice on every important matter. But the Holy Spirit will be with you forever. Jesus promised it. The Spirit will act as your advocate and counselor, like a personal attorney ready to be consulted whenever you wish. And His only fee is that you give Him your heart.

Why do I love the Holy Spirit? I love Him because He comforts me when I'm discouraged; He whispers advice when I'm confused; He strengthens me to witness about Jesus when I'm hesitant; He guides me to choose the right thing and then gives me joy in doing it.

In the canon of the Mass, the priest proclaims that Jesus sent us the Holy Spirit so that "we might live no longer for ourselves but for Him, to complete His work on earth and bring us the fullness of grace." Left to ourselves, we can be pretty selfish and petty. But the magnificent Holy Spirit lifts us out of our own smallness and sweeps us into the greatness of God and His perspective.

Then there are the gifts of the Holy Spirit! I was so foolish to think that jewelry was the only gift I'd receive at Confirmation. Believe me, Peter, the Lord has great gifts, spiritual gifts, in store for you as you open yourself fully to His Spirit. You're embarking on an exciting adventure with a wonderful God.

On the day you were born, Fr. Cohen received a Scripture passage for you: "The Spirit of the Lord is upon me because the Lord has anointed me." Yes, Peter Michael John Mansfield, the Spirit of the Lord is upon you, and He will come upon you in an even greater measure in Confirmation. Receive His anointing! He plans to accomplish in you "infinitely more than you can ask or imagine!" (cf. Ephesians 3:20). And always remember: I love you!!

Mom

The Prayer of Children

"Why does Jesus like lasagna so much?", asked my little girl one day.

I was stunned. Even if I'm of Italian descent and love this pasta dish, I'd never claim that the Lord had a preference for Italian food!

But my daughter was convinced He did. "Mom, I know Jesus loves lasagna. Don't you know that's why we sing about it at Church. "Lasagna! Lasagna! Lasagna in the highest!"

Her logic was flawless, even if her linguistics weren't! At least she was paying attention at Mass. In fact, my husband and I are continually amazed at how attentive small children can be to spiritual things. Don't fail to expose your youngsters to prayer, no matter how young they are. While not every Catholic family may opt to bring their little ones to Mass, every family *can* teach prayer within the home. Visits to churches and shrines provide another opportunity to introduce children to the things of God.

I'll never forget our visit to a retreat center dedicated to Mary when our two boys were little. On the beautiful grounds there were several statues depicting Mary under different titles. We stopped at each statue of Our Lady and prayed a "Hail Mary." Then we explained to our sons about Guadalupe, Lourdes, and Fatima. When our little "Marian pilgrimage" was over, six-year-old Mark asked in confusion, "Does Our Lady of Guadalupe turn into Our Lady of Lourdes and then turn into

Our Lady of Fatima or what? Which Our Lady is Our Lady?"
My husband and I had some explaining to do!

There are at least two types of prayer you may teach your
little ones—rote prayer and spontaneous prayer. You'd be
surprised how quickly our young children have been able to
memorize prayers such as the "Our Father" and "Hail Mary."
My husband has taken the lead in teaching the children these
prayers at night before they go to bed. We kneel for a few
moments and pray together. Even if they don't understand the
meaning of all the words yet, there is a great value in helping
our little ones enter into the prayer of the Church. I must
confess to you that I've only recently learned the prayer "Soul
of Christ." When my four-year-old child committed it to
memory, I knew I had no excuse! After our prayers we get in
a circle and give a "Family Hug" which usually ends in giggles
and a chase around the room.

Spontaneous prayer, talking to Jesus in our own words, is
equally as important. Here's where young children are often
way ahead of us adults because of their confidence and trust.
Our youngsters have asked Jesus to do things we didn't have
faith for ourselves, and He's answered their prayers.

For instance, one day my husband had a headache and our
young son, Peter, about six at the time, knew it. "I'll pray for
you, Dad," offered Peter. He put his hand on his dad's shoulder
and said simply, "Jesus, please take Daddy's headache away.
Thank you, Jesus." In the next breath he inquired, "Is it gone,
Dad?" Now that's faith! When Peter found out the headache
was persisting, he persisted and prayed again. Before long, the
headache lifted!

Whenever a member of our family is ill or in special need, we
try to pray for him with the laying on of hands. This may be
done very simply, yet it has great power to unleash the healing
love of Jesus. My friend's one-year-old hurt her foot and kept

holding it out to her mom with the plea, "Or it, or it!" My friend finally realized the child wanted her to pray "over it!" She placed her hand on the child's foot, prayed, and the little one was content. Lay hands in prayer on your children and let them lay hands on you.

Another beautiful way to share prayer with small children is by giving a blessing. One of my most cherished childhood memories is of receiving my mother's blessing at night. She'd trace a small sign of the cross on my forehead with her thumb. This is a simple but profound way of claiming our children for Christ and marking them with His cross. All our pre-schoolers have loved to reverse roles and give us their blessing.

Young children really respond to ceremonies marking the liturgical year within the home, too. They love the Advent wreath and Jesse tree symbols in preparation for Christmas. For each child's feast day we honor him with a small gift and recall the virtues of his saint. We had to tell Marie-Thérèse that in addition to October 1 for St. Thérèse, she could only choose one of Mary's feast days as her own. Otherwise, her brothers would complain of unfair treatment.

At times we've prayed a novena together as a family for a special intention. Invariably, the youngest child will remind us to pray by distributing the prayer cards. He holds his own upside down, but his prayer of babble is powerful nonetheless! Sometimes we pray a decade of the rosary as a family. The smallest child loves to pass out rosary beads to everyone with the command, "Pray!". I know of families where the rosary is prayed in common daily.

Remember to teach your little ones to offer up their sacrifices and sufferings to Jesus. Again, I've been amazed at how quickly young children can grasp this profound concept of redemptive suffering. Let them be familiar with the crucifix by having one in your home. Explain that when we offer up our hurts together with Jesus, this is a form of prayer. One day my seven-year-old had a fever and I reminded him to offer up his sickness to the Lord. "Oh, Mom, I did that right away," came the reply. If only I could be so quick to unite my sufferings to the cross of Jesus!

A final word about teaching small children to pray. Entrust your family to Mary, the mother of Jesus and our mother too. Ask her to take you into her heart as you pass through this life and keep you always close to the heart of her Son, Jesus. She helped form the prayer of the Child Jesus and of the apostles as well. She will surely be a mother to our families by teaching us all to pray.

 Opportunities

When I was newly baptized in the Holy Spirit I eagerly welcomed every opportunity to give witness to what God had done in my life. The simplest question from an unsuspecting stranger would prompt a detailed version of my personal testimony. Even though my zeal wasn't always enlightened, God blessed my efforts to evangelize.

During that zealous period I carried my huge, hardbound Jerusalem Bible under my arm while traveling, much to my father's chagrin. When he asked why I didn't put it in a paper bag, I simply explained that it was a wonderful way to start a conversation about Jesus. People couldn't help but notice it!

As time went by, I lost some of my eagerness to share the Good News. Many an opportunity on a plane, in a restroom, on a beach, in a grocery store or doctor's office, passed me by because I was too tired, busy, or preoccupied. "Make the most of the present opportunity," Scripture exhorts us (Ephesians 5:16). Each day we are surrounded by people who are longing for the loving touch of Jesus that comes through us if only we take the time to reach out. Recently I met two people who reminded me of this truth.

My husband and I were waiting for our plane after a conference, when I happened into a casual conversation with a young woman seated nearby. In the midst of our small talk, I had a sense from the Lord that she was suffering in her family life. Before I knew it, this woman began pouring her heart out to me. She had just suffered a miscarriage and had been told she had little chance of ever bearing a child. Then her twin brother died suddenly. As she spoke, it was natural to put my arm around her in comfort and offer to pray with her. She knew the Lord, but at that moment she needed the reassurance of His love for her. Her gratitude for the prayer was genuine, and we parted with an embrace. She has written to me since to thank me.

Once on board the plane, my husband and I began to talk together about the good things the Lord had done for us during the conference. An older man seated next to my husband, Al, looked unfriendly, and I concluded that our conversation was annoying him.

We didn't exchange a word with the man until the plane landed. Then he leaned over and said, "Pardon me. I hope you don't mind, but I overheard your conversation about Christ. Will you please pray for me? My son is ill, and I'm terribly worried about him."

Immediately, we joined hands and prayed for the boy. This gentleman, whom I thought to be unfriendly, was in reality worried about his son. He was just waiting for us to share Christ with him. How grateful he was for that brief moment of prayer!

As we go about our daily lives, let's ask the Holy Spirit to help us "make the most of the present opportunity" to share the Good News with those we meet. The Lord will use us if we're willing.

 Hurricane Season

When I was growing up in New Jersey, I never really experienced the fury of a hurricane. But after moving South I began to understand what devastation a hurricane could bring to those who live close to the water. During drives along the Mississippi Gulf Coast, my husband has shown me remnants of many buildings that once graced the shore.

In 1969, as Hurricane Camille hovered over the Gulf of Mexico, people in coastal towns were urged to evacuate. Despite repeated warnings, many residents decided to remain. They had weathered other storms, they said, and they would ride this one out as well. I know of one woman who stubbornly refused to leave her home until the rising waters forced her to flee to a neighbor's second floor apartment. After the trauma of that experience, she needed no persuasion to heed hurricane warnings in the future.

It was not just stubbornness, however, that kept some Mississippi residents in their homes during Hurricane Camille. There were about 20 people who took a mocking attitude toward the threat of impending danger. They were so sure that destruction could never touch them, that they had the audacity to throw a "hurricane party." As the storm approached the coast they sang, danced, and drank, ignoring the news reports. When Camille's tidal wave hit the shore all 20 were killed as their host's brick house collapsed upon them. To this day only the cement foundation remains as a grim reminder of the pride and arrogance of those who would not heed a warning.

Hurricanes like Camille don't usually come every year, but during a recent hurricane season on the Gulf Coast, we weathered three major hurricanes in a three month period. Camille taught us a lesson. During Hurricane Elena, September, 1985, nearly a million people were evacuated. The newscasters kept residents informed about the progress of the storm, and those in danger were able to prepare and quickly move to safer areas. Although there was extensive property damage, only three people died. Considering that the winds reached a force of 125 miles per hour, it's remarkable that so few lost their lives. The key to survival was in heeding the warnings given by the weathermen.

Of course there are those who accuse weathermen of using scare tactics and inciting fear to force people to evacuate. There are those who feel that too much time is devoted to covering the development of storms by newscasters. Some people still insist that no storm can ever touch them. Yet countless lives have been saved because weather warnings are given and heeded.

As hurricane season comes around each year in the South, I can't help but think of those "newscasters" and "weathermen" of the spiritual order who are reading the signs of the times and issuing warnings today: *Repent! Be converted to God! Fast! Pray! Make peace among yourselves! Beg for God's mercy on the world!* These are Scriptural messages, always in season, but proclaimed in our times with a greater urgency than before.

Perhaps these messages of repentance, conversion, fasting, prayer and peace are as unwelcome as a weather report about an approaching hurricane, but thank God there are those who will faithfully issue a warning when it's needed. May you and I have the wisdom to heed such warnings and so find safety.

A Spelling Lesson

Those of us who attended grade school before sophisticated audio-visuals, remember our one fun activity—the old-fashioned spelling bee. It was always exciting toward the end of the bee when words like *congratulations, occasion* and *privilege* came up. (I still misspell the word *privilege* much to my husband's chagrin. It looks so naked without a "d" in it!)

I thought spelling lessons were far behind me until one day last summer when I flipped on the car radio to a Christian station. I had it on only long enough to hear a family counselor say, "Our children spell LOVE like this: T-I-M-E." Just a few days later I realized it was not at all by chance that I had received this spelling lesson.

My two older sons had foregone sports at the playground after my baby's birth. As summer approached, we told them they could sign up for baseball and they were thrilled. One of my boys came home from the playground and threw the baseball schedule on the table dejectedly. "I just want you to know how important this is to me," he muttered. Once I examined the schedule, I understood the problem.

Almost every Wednesday night he was scheduled to play. Wednesday is our prayer meeting night and I was anxious to get back to the meetings after missing several months because of the baby. The spelling lesson echoed loud and clear in my mind. "Our children spell love T-l-M-E."

"It's alright, you can still play," I reassured my boys.

"But what about your prayer meeting?" my oldest son asked.

(Gulp!) "I'll just miss it for the summer," I replied.

Suddenly his whole attitude changed. "It doesn't seem fair for you to miss the prayer meeting because of baseball, Mom," he said. But I insisted.

Many times as I carted my baby to the playground at 9:30 p.m. I reminded myself, "Our children spell love T-I-M-E." And you know, they really did get the message. More than anything else I could have done that summer, allowing them to play baseball was a communication of my love. I had to assure my friends at the prayer meeting that my absence was not due to "backsliding." I was watching my boys sliding into home plate instead!

The experts confirm the connection between loving and spending time. A good friend, Jim Kelly, is executive director of Covenant House New Orleans, a shelter for homeless youth. Jim's experience has convinced him that parents need to spend more time building a relationship with their children. The young people at Covenant House come from a variety of situations, but they all share a common hunger. They're starved for love and attention. If their parents had taken the time to make them feel loved, they may not have resorted to life on the street. Jim believes that parents need to invest quantity as well as quality time with their young people. This means getting priorities straight. In his words, "God first, then the family, then the job—not the reverse order."

Have you seen the TV commercial with the little boy standing next to his mom while she's working at her desk?

"Mommy...Mommy...Whatcha doin'?"

"I'm busy, Honey," comes the distracted reply.

"Mommy...Whatcha writin' in that book?" He gives a little tug at her sleeve.

"I'm writing my schedule of meetings with important people." She goes back to work.

"Mommy, is *my* name in that book?"

Suddenly the mother stops and really looks at the child. She puts down her pen and hugs him. I don't know about you, but a message like that hits home where I live.

We all have numerous responsibilities vying for our time and attention. Occasionally, we have to say no to our children's needs in order to give ourselves to others who also have a claim on us. But that doesn't absolve us of our responsibility to search out ways to spend time with our children.

Something that's worked well for us is scheduling a time with each child. Every other month, Al brings one of our sons to Saturday morning Mass and then to breakfast. They call it a "Headship Meeting." It's a special time to talk and just be together. This is often followed by a work project.

Marie-Thérèse and I have a "Girls' Day Out"—to shop, run errands, or attend a Disney movie. (We always sneak in a frozen yogurt, but don't tell the boys!) Recently, Al decided to take our daughter out to breakfast. She enjoyed it so much she even wrote him a thank you note!

During supper we always ask each child to share a high point and a low point of the day. It's a simple way to encourage communication.

Find what works in your family situation and do it. It's crucial to the health of your family. Remember, our children spell love like this: T-I-M-E.

Vacation Alert

For years I'd been longing to attend a conference on smocking and fine hand sewing, but the cost of travel, lodging and tuition was prohibitive. To my delight, just such a conference came to New Orleans several months ago and my husband suggested that I consider it my birthday/Christmas/Mother's Day gift all rolled into one. I happily obliged. Spending a few days learning new stitching techniques and being inspired by the beauty of "fabric masterpieces," is my idea of relaxation. Some people recreate or "re-create" themselves by travel, sports or music; instead I pick up a needle and thread. This conference was to be my personal vacation, a time to "get away from it all." Little did I realize that the Lord would meet me at the School of Needle Arts with a lesson of His own.

Although several hundred people were in attendance at the school, there were two women who always landed by my side. One was a lovely young designer from Guatemala; the other woman was from Maine. We found ourselves in the same classes, at the same lunch table and even visiting the rest room at the same time. "You're sticking to me like glue!", the girl from Maine exclaimed.

The young designer, Annabella, had never been to New Orleans, and during the conference we were beset by a mild hurricane. She was frightened by the weather and I tried to ease her anxieties. When we parted, she hugged and kissed me as though I had done her a great service. In reality, all I did was simply make her feel welcome.

Talking with Diane, the woman from Maine, I discovered we were both married in 1973 and our four children were the same ages. Diane and I seemed to have a lot in common until I mentioned my involvement with church work. She told me emphatically, "I haven't stepped foot inside a church since my wedding day!" Diane made a few more remarks about the Church that indicated she felt hurt and rejected. I tried to assure her that God's love was still available, but her manner made it clear that she wasn't open to being evangelized. I didn't pursue the conversation any further. But when the conference ended, I offered Diane a copy of *New Covenant*, the Catholic magazine I wrote for at the time. Diane took the magazine rather readily. "I'll read it on the plane," she said. "Who knows, maybe this will help me get some religion again." It was just a seed planted, very gently. I'll probably never see Diane again, but God's grace will continue to pursue her.

As I headed for home, thoroughly refreshed by the time apart, I felt as though the Lord wanted to speak to me. His message was something like this. "Patti, remember to be for Me. You came for one purpose, to get away from it all, but I had another plan. I wanted you to make My presence known to the people you met."

I then realized that Annabella and Diane were by my side for a reason. It was a powerful reminder that there is never a vacation or break from our call to make the Lord known and loved. Whether through active evangelism, simple kindness, prayer, or a friendly smile, the Lord expects us to be His instruments. He desires to use us, even in the midst of recreation if only we are willing.

Two friends of mine, Hulda and Corinne, have learned this lesson well. They spent their vacation last year taking a bus tour through the Ozarks. During the trip a woman seated across the aisle took sick with chills and fever. Although my friends didn't know her personally, they were concerned.

Unobtrusively, Hulda reached her hand over to touch the woman's foot and prayed in silence for healing. The sick woman couldn't feel Hulda's touch from under a mountain of covers. But within no time, the fever broke, and she began telling everyone how much better she felt.

"Sure you feel better," piped up another passenger, "that woman next to you prayed for you. I saw her!" All eyes turned to Hulda as she nodded her confession. Immediately another passenger with a special need made her way up the aisle of the bus and knelt before Hulda and Corinne. "Please pray for me now," she asked humbly, kneeling in the middle of the bus.

Isn't it beautiful that in the midst of a vacation, Hulda and Corinne were willing to let their light shine? Because of their courage, God used them to touch other lives with His healing love.

The Lord wants to remind you to bring His presence into every situation. He would say to you, *"Be for Me. Be My man. Be My woman. Be My child. Wherever you go, whatever you do, remember to be for Me."*

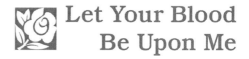# Let Your Blood Be Upon Me

What do you do when you're fearful, worried or anxious? After identifying the source of my fears, I usually try to take some action. There might be a need for repentance, for inner healing, a change of direction, or counsel to alleviate the distress. But one thing I always do is to pray for the protection of the blood of Jesus. I'd like to share with you what I've learned about it as I've tried to "walk in the Spirit" over the years.

When I was first baptized in the Spirit, I remember singing hymns that honored the name and the blood of Jesus at our prayer meetings. The power of God was quickly made manifest when we proclaimed clearly and with conviction that we were gathered in the name of Jesus. What a wonderful freedom of worship we had when we asked for the blood of the Lamb to wash us clean. "O the blood of Jesus, it cleanses white as snow." We sang it. We believed it. We experienced it.

I came to realize this truth: "Our battle is not against human forces but against the principalities and powers, the rulers of this world of darkness, the evil spirits in the regions above" (Ephesians 6:12). In order to do spiritual warfare, we need to be armed with the word of God, calling on the name of Jesus and pleading his precious blood. Not all the battles we fight are spiritual warfare; there's the world and the flesh to overcome. But when I am bombarded by fears and anxieties, I've learned to take up "the whole armor of God," including the power in the precious blood. I'm surprised when I meet Christians who don't avail themselves of this practice.

A religious sister once told me how she was tormented by feelings of dread and foreboding with no apparent reason. She had never thought of praying for healing and deliverance through the blood of Christ. This may not have been the only way to combat her fears, but it was certainly a powerful means to do so. I shared with her how my husband and I pray invoking the blood of Christ.

Every time we receive the Eucharist, we believe we are receiving the body and blood of Christ. As Catholics, this is the best time to appropriate the healing and deliverance Jesus has for us in His blood. What does Scripture tell us about Christ's blood? The blood of the Lamb cleanses us from sin (I John 1:17). The blood gives us eternal life (John 6:54). The blood fills us with confidence to approach God (Hebrews 10:19). The blood sanctifies us (Hebrews 13:12). The blood helps us conquer the enemy (Revelation 12:11). What treasures are ours for the asking through the precious blood!

Al and I frequently meditate on these Scripture passages and pray the Church's Litany to the Precious Blood. Every night, Al prays with our children, "Lord, we place Your precious blood upon the doorposts of our home to protect us from all harm." Just as the blood of the Lamb protected the Israelites from the angel of death, so does the blood of Jesus, the Lamb of God, serve as our protection when we appropriate it for ourselves and our loved ones.

In the *Dialogue* of St. Catherine of Siena, it's striking how often God speaks to her of the precious blood. The first time I read through the Father's words to Catherine the *Dialogue*, I began to underline every time the Father mentioned the precious blood of Jesus. It's on almost every page. Catherine has even been called by some, "The Prophetess of the Blood." The Father said to her, *"No one need fear any battle or temptation of the devil that may come, for I have made you strong and given your wills power in the blood of My Son."*

Priests are to be specially honored because they are the keepers of the keys of His blood. I would add that in this moment in the Church when priests need so much strengthening and spiritual support, we should invoke the protection of the precious blood upon them often.

Inspired by Catherine's love for the precious blood, I've been led to invoke the blood more and more often in daily life. The words used to condemn Jesus during his passion have become words of love for me as I pray: "O Lord, let Your blood be on me." Instead of a judgment against me, I pray that the blood of Jesus be my protection and freedom. "O Lord, let Your blood be on me and on my home. Let Your blood be on me and on my children, and on my work, my car, my travels," and so on.

Recently I was praying this way before a meeting to be held in our home. I rarely have any visual image when I pray, but this time I did. As I looked up, I was startled by the image of red blood dripping from the ceiling of our living room. The Lord's voice deep within me seemed to say, "When you ask me to do this, I really do it." Never before had I seen the blood, but in that instance, Jesus wanted me to know the reality of His blood being poured forth for our protection. And, there's power in the blood! Take up all the weapons of spiritual warfare the Lord has provided. Plead the blood of Jesus and be set free!

"To Him who loved us and freed us from our sins by His own blood, who made us a royal nation of priests in the service of His God and Father—to Him be glory and power forever and ever. Amen" (Revelation 1:5).

God Is Greater

"Did you ever feel like giving up?" my friend asked me over the phone. Encouraged by my affirmative hum, she continued.

"Well, I do! I've been fighting with the Lord for weeks about the things that have been happening in my life. I feel worn out and worn down by difficulties. In fact, I even told the Lord to forget what I said years ago about wanting to be a saint, to be holy. Scratch that! I just don't think I've got what it takes. I mean, I'm willing to work for the Lord and serve Him, but it's these humiliations, misunderstandings, strained relationships and uncertainties about the future—I'm just not sure I can hack it!"

Sound familiar? It did to me. In fact, I've been amazed at how many brothers and sisters near and far are experiencing similar trials. It seems like everywhere I turn, I meet Christians who are facing grave personal problems, difficulties with family, ministry or community. What's happening? It's as though a shaking is going on in the lives of God's people and only what is pure, holy and built on Him will endure. God is after something in His servants. He's getting our attention. Remember this admonition from the book of Sirach? I shared it with my friend.

> *"My son, when you come to serve the Lord, prepare yourself for trials. Be sincere of heart and steadfast, undisturbed in time of adversity. Cling to Him, forsake Him not; thus will your future be great. Accept whatever befalls you, in crushing misfortune be patient; for in fire gold is tested and worthy men in the crucible of humiliation"* (Sirach 2:1-5).

My friend knew just how hot that crucible can be! That's why she was complaining. Later my friend told me that when she got through fighting with the Lord, He asked her this question: "Now that you're finished complaining, what are you going to do? You've got to make a new decision. Will you follow Me or not?"

This was a moment of truth for her. Humbled in His presence, with the knowledge that only Jesus is worthy of such love, my friend echoed the words of the disciples long ago. "Lord, to whom shall we go? You have the words of eternal life. We have come to believe; we are convinced that You are God's holy one" (John 6:68-69).

Like Mary, my friend said "Yes." "Be it done unto me." And that settled it for her. She decided anew to "cling to Him and forsake Him not." No matter what it may cost. No matter how things may look. No matter where He may lead.

What's God after in His servants? What has He been trying to teach us? My friend and I agreed that in our lives the Lord wants more than faithful service. *He wants our hearts!* He wants us to be so identified with Him, so united to Him, so much in love with Him, that our joy derives from belonging to Him, whatever the circumstances may be.

What about you? Is your life being shaken? Are things around you falling apart? Are you fighting with the Lord? Have you made a fresh decision to go with Jesus to Calvary and beyond? In the midst of your difficulties stands the Master, arms outstretched, saying "Come follow Me." He's waiting for your response.

Years ago I was finding it hard to say yes to God because of a devastating disappointment. My husband received a word for me which helped me see beyond the difficulty of the moment. It may help you, in the midst of your struggle, to push through to surrender. Al said simply, "God is greater."

"Greater than what?", I retorted.

"You name it. Fill in the blank," he replied. "God is greater than this disappointment. He's greater than our hopes and dreams. God is greater than our experience, our understanding, our categories of how He works. He's greater than our family, our community or ministry. God is greater than our hearts and He knows everything."

Somehow that word changed my perspective. On my refrigerator I posted a sign that read, *God Is Greater*! and kept it there all year to minister to me. And do you know what? As I focused more on God and less on my troubles, He brought me into a deeper relationship with Him than I had before. I can now look back and thank Him for the very disappointment that led me to discover Him in a new way. It's true, my friends. May you learn it for yourselves. *God is greater!*

You Can Do It!

"You what?!" I exclaimed.

I was on the phone with my friend Fr. Jim Ferry during a week-long visit home to New Jersey in 1968. He had just informed me that he'd arranged for me to speak at a church nearby. The flyers were already out; everything was all set. He just hadn't gotten around to checking with me ahead of time. How could I object at this late date?

Maybe the reason why Fr. Jim hadn't asked my permission, was that he knew I'd refuse. I frequently protested that I didn't have enough training to speak about the Lord. To which Fr. Jim would jokingly reply that the Holy Spirit would touch people through me even if all I did was to read from the phone book. Talk about pumping confidence into someone! "You can do it," he'd say. I will be eternally grateful to Fr. Jim for his great faith that God wanted to use me. If he hadn't pushed and prodded me into ministry, I would never be involved in Christian service to the extent that I am today.

And I'm not the only person who can say this. Just recently I received a beautiful testimony from another one of Fr. Jim's protégées, Janis Clarke of Montreal, Canada. I want to share it with you as an illustration of the power of loving affirmation—calling forth the best in others to the glory of God. Fr. Jim did that so well! It's also a delightful illustration of the communion of saints—small "s." Even after death we can help one another through our prayer.

Here's Janis' story: When she arrived in New Jersey in the fall of 1985, Fr. Jim took her under his wing and introduced her to the people at St. Antoninus parish in Newark where he was pastor. One day Fr. Jim discovered that Janis had a gift for singing. At the next prayer meeting he put her on the spot and requested a song. After that Fr. Jim would call on Janis frequently to sing at various gatherings of God's people. Janis usually felt nervous and unprepared, but she trusted that the Lord was speaking through Fr. Jim's invitation to sing.

At one point Fr. Jim told Janis this: "It's better to use your gifts and struggle with pride than to bury your gifts." He went on to encourage this young woman to place her musical abilities in the service of the Lord. "You can do it, Janis."

Not long afterward Janis returned home to Montreal. Because of her work in youth ministry she was straining her voice and losing her classical technique in singing. She cried out to the Lord in frustration praying, "Oh, Lord, if Fr. Jim's words of encouragement were really from You, then why does it seem that every door to serving You in song is closing?" It was then that she received news of Fr. Ferry's death.

At first she felt sorrow because she'd never see her friend again, but then she realized that she no longer had to travel to New Jersey to experience his love and support. The next morning she got down on her knees in prayer and said, "Fr. Jim, please talk to Jesus about this whole singing thing. If I continue in youth ministry and don't get back to singing lessons, I'll wreck my voice. Please remind the Lord that I need voice lessons and the money to pay for them as well."

Then she stepped out in faith and called one of the best voice teachers in town. (She remembered Fr. Jim's constant admonition "*Think Big!*") The teacher agreed to audition her on St. Patrick's Day. (Janis thought of Fr. Jim's great love for the Irish.) The instructor wasn't very encouraging and told

Janis there were no openings for new students at the time. When the teacher mentioned the cost of the lessons, Janis swallowed hard and replied, "Money won't be a problem." In actuality, Janis could barely make ends meet, but she was believing that Fr. Jim had taken up her need with Jesus. Her faith was rewarded.

Two weeks later Janis received a money order in the mail marked *"Anonymous Gift."* The money order had been issued on St. Patrick's Day and it contained enough money to pay for almost two years of voice lessons! The following week the instructor called to say she had an opening after all. And so Janis began her voice lessons in preparation for a ministry of song which will bring glory to God. Alleluia! Or better, "Hooray!", as Fr. Jim would say.

Janis is convinced, and I am too, that our mutual friend, Fr. Jim Ferry, was up to his old shenanigans from his new vantage point in God's heavenly kingdom. Witness the power of loving affirmation to call forth gifts of service! Witness the power of intercessory prayer in the communion of saints! God is so good!

A Kind Answer

I was so delighted to find out that Karin Sefcik Treiber, my friend from college days, was coming to visit. We had become like sisters in Christ, sharing our joys and sorrows while we were in school together. For years since graduation we had interceded for each other concerning God's will regarding our vocations. Each of us wanted to be married, but we knew that it would only come about if it were the Lord's will. There was a time of waiting and trusting, learning to walk each day with Jesus. I had already been married several years when Karin called with her good news. The Lord had brought a wonderful man into her life. We thanked God for His faithfulness.

To celebrate the joyous occasion of seeing Karin and her husband, Bob, my husband and I decided to bring them to one of the finest restaurants in New Orleans. The "Underground Gourmet" ranked this restaurant with four stars—excellent food and drink, elegant decor and courteous service! We were sure that everything would be just perfect.

Imagine my disappointment when we entered the restaurant and were greeted halfheartedly by a busy host. The wait for a table seemed interminable. When we were finally seated, it wasn't in the Garden Room, the Red Room or Gold Room, but off in a noisy corner of the bar! But the worst part of it all was the waiter. To say he was unfriendly would be an understatement. The man was downright rude! He seemed to feel we were imposing on his time by just being there.

At first I was embarrassed and then angry at the treatment we were receiving. I was almost ready to make known my irritation by asking for another table when my friend, Karin, caught my eye. "It's all right," she said softly.

What happened in the next hour or so was a marvel to behold. Each time this gruff waiter appeared, Karin smiled at him sweetly and said something kind. She went out of her way to compliment him even in the midst of his unwilling service. Instead of allowing his rude manner to spoil our joy, she seemed bent on drawing him into the celebration. Karin's kindness to the waiter certainly saved me embarrassment but it did much more than that.

By the end of the meal, Karin had so completely won him over, that he seemed like a different man. Before we left he picked a fresh flower from the table nearby and handed to her. "Have a good day, Miss! Enjoy your visit!" I could hardly believe it! What a transformation!

As we left the restaurant, Karin handed me the flower. "It's for you, Dear. Thanks for bringing us here to celebrate. It was so special," she said while hugging me.

"How did you manage to change that waiter, Karin?" I asked as we left. Her answer came from the Scriptures. "A mild answer calms wrath, but a harsh word stirs up anger" (Proverbs 15:1). I wanted to change the waiter by moving away from him. She changed the waiter by moving closer to him. What a lesson I learned from my friend that day in the restaurant.

Kindness, that fruit of the Holy Spirit within us, can touch and change lives. Kindness in words and kindness in deeds can transform situations before our eyes. To manifest kindness is to show forth the loving presence of Jesus to others. And the presence of Jesus has power to transform. In Sirach 6:5 we read, "A kind mouth multiplies friends, and gracious lips prompt friendly greetings." Again in Proverbs 15:4, "A soothing tongue is a tree of life."

When it would have been so easy to take offense, Karin chose instead to respond with kindness. That kindness did calm wrath (mine!). It touched hearts, made a new friend, and added to the joy of our celebration. The glory of God was revealed because one person chose to be kind. May you and I go and do likewise.

P.S. Karin Sefcik Treiber died in December, 2012, having spent the last months of her life showing exquisite attention to everyone around her. A truly selfless woman who died a truly holy death! Rest in peace, dear friend!

Teach Us to Pray

"How can we get our kids to pray?"

This is one of the questions I'm frequently asked by young parents who are eager to instill faith in their children. It's been said that religion is caught, not taught, and there's certainly truth in that statement. We've found our small children eager to "catch" the faith, that is, to know and love the Lord, if we make our home environment a place where Jesus is honored. One of the fundamentals of passing on the faith to our children, is creating an atmosphere of prayer.

Years ago when my son, Peter, was a toddler, I arranged to take my daily prayer time in the afternoon while he watched Sesame Street on television. One particularly sleepy day I kept dozing off as I sat in my rocker with the Bible. "This will never do," I scolded myself as I got out of the rocker and down on my knees. Bending low, hands folded, eyes closed, I tried to pray once more. Within a matter of minutes I sensed a presence in the room. No, it wasn't an angel or even an apparition, just my little boy, Peter! As I opened my eyes, there he was, crouched down in exactly the same position I was. Peter's nose almost touched mine as he whispered in a sweet voice, "What are we praying about today, Mom?"

This incident spoke volumes to me about teaching small children to pray. Peter not only wanted to be close to me. He wanted to enter into my prayer. Despite my sleepiness and distractions, my example in prayer was a powerful tool in drawing Peter to seek God, too!

I love to picture the child Jesus, the Word made flesh, learning to pray in the home of Mary and Joseph. Surely there must have been times of family prayer, times when He observed His earthly parents seeking God, times when He was instructed in the faith of His fathers.

If we really want to pass on the faith to our children, we must be men and women of prayer ourselves. Please establish a daily prayer time, if you don't already have one. To communicate the reality of God's love and power to your children, you need to drink daily of the living waters of His presence yourself. Set aside at least 15–30 minutes of quiet time to pray and read God's word. If you can possibly attend Mass daily or several times a week, do so.

For small children to relate to Jesus in a natural way, they need to understand that He is as close to them as you are. Let your home be permeated by His presence. How can you do this? In our own family, because most of our relatives live in other states, we are accustomed to keeping them present to our children through photos, stories and special visits. In the same way, you can make Jesus a family member by speaking to your little ones about Him during the day, reading children's Bible stories at nap time and having pictures or statues of Him in your home.

One of my most vivid childhood memories involved a brief encounter with a relative who pressed me to her side as she read a Bible story. Through the beautiful illustrations of the book, Jesus seemed to come right off the page and into my heart. The warmth of her love as she held me close, made it easy for me to believe that Jesus loved me too. Don't underestimate the power of God's grace which can break into a young life as you do something as simple as reading a Bible story!

Above our kitchen table we have a collection of icons and drawings of Jesus, Mary and the saints along with a crucifix.

Our baby, Patrick, was not even one year old when he began climbing on a chair to touch the pictures of Jesus and Mary. On many occasions I'd walk into the kitchen and find him kissing and chewing on the corner of the icon of Jesus. "Je, Je," he'd say with enthusiasm as I tried to pry it out of his fingers. In his own little baby way he was showing honor and love for Jesus as he kissed the icon. Small children will show their love for God if they are surrounded by reminders of His presence and encouraged to relate to Him. Of course, I would have been happier if Patrick had blown a kiss to Jesus rather than chew His image!

And don't forget the influence of good Christian music in bringing the presence of God to your family. Years ago we used to play Gregorian chant during meals. (The children called it "Agorian Chance!") In recent years we've used more popular Christian music including delightful children's music. Our two-year-old loves the music of Psalty the Songbook and insists on singing and dancing to Christian music almost every day. I'm his favorite dance partner! When I play praise music in the car, his little hands lift up in worship. Visit a Christian bookstore and invest in some music which will transform your home into a place of praise and prayer.

Just like the disciples of Jesus long ago, our little disciples in the family are asking us, "Teach us to pray." This is an awesome responsibility. Let's apply ourselves to the task with the help of the Holy Spirit and rejoice as these little ones come to know and love the Lord.

In the Stillness of the Night

"In the stillness of the night when the world was asleep the almighty Word leaped down." These words from a song we often sing at prayer meetings are a paraphrased version of Wisdom 18:14-16. They come readily to mind each year when we celebrate the birth of Jesus Our Savior who came forth from Mary's womb in the stillness of the night. We celebrate His birth each year by exchanging gifts with those we love as we remember the greatest of all gifts—Jesus Christ Himself.

One December many years ago I felt that the Lord was offering me a special Christmas gift—the gift of deeper faith. My first response to the idea of a new gift of faith was one of joy. Surely growing in faith is of utmost importance in our spiritual lives for "without faith it is impossible to please God" (Hebrews 11:6). Somehow I naively expected to wake up one day energized by a new depth of faith. This didn't happen. Instead, the Lord intended to extend this Christmas gift throughout the entire new year.

When the holidays were over, my journey into a deeper walk of faith was just beginning. I noticed I still had a nagging cough which had lingered after a bout with the flu. Although I tried to ignore it, the cough grew worse. When I finally saw a doctor he told me I had pneumonia and prescribed medication and bed rest. Since I had a baby who was still nursing at the time and up frequently at night, my mother flew in from out of town to care for me.

Week after week my lungs would not clear. Discouragement set in. I regretted causing inconvenience to my husband and mother while I was recuperating, but I really needed their help. Each day as I tried to pray it was such a struggle to overcome these feelings of discouragement.

When I was finally over the pneumonia, my resistance was so low that I was prone to other infections. For the next few months I seemed to be sick most of the time. Then came some minor eye surgery, followed by another hospital stay to remove a lump which proved to be benign. None of these physical problems was really serious. It was the fact that they were following one upon another that was wearing me down. I knew the Lord was with me in the midst of it all, even though it was often difficult to feel His presence. Thank God that by the end of that year I was well and strong again.

As December approached again I remembered that the Lord had promised me a gift of deeper faith the Christmas before. Then I realized that through all these experiences He was indeed providing me with opportunities to grow in loving trust of Him. The faith I so desired was meant to be strengthened by passing through some trials and difficulties which would help me mature as a Christian and learn to cling to Him in everything.

It was "in the stillness of the night," when there was darkness all around that the Almighty Word leaped down that first Christmas. In our lives it is often in the stillness of the night when all seems dark, discouraging, and hopeless that God is deeply at work in our souls. First He shows us our need for Him, then He meets our need with a fresh revelation of Himself!

My problems that year were minor compared to what many of you may be facing right now in the stillness of the night. Perhaps it is the pain of a broken marriage, concern over the welfare of a child, sickness, loss of a loved one, or lack of a job. Remember that our faithful God is very near you. Nothing can *ever* separate you from His love. God is able to supply *every* need of yours fully according to His riches and glory in Christ Jesus (Philippians 4:19). That's His word. You can stake your life on it. He will never fail you. Your faith will be strengthened as you pass through your difficulties.

St. Peter tells us, "You may for a time have to suffer the distress of many trials; but this is so that your faith, which is *more precious than the passing splendor of fire-tried gold*, may by its genuineness lead to praise, glory and honor when Jesus Christ appears" (I Peter 1:6-7).

Do not let your hearts be troubled or afraid, no matter what your circumstances may be. My prayer is that you will cling to Jesus in the stillness of the night so that when day breaks, He may bring you forth as pure gold!

Taming the Tongue

You've probably heard the joke about the three fastest means of communication: telegraph, telephone and tell-a-woman! While we women might wince, we've got to admit that most of us do like to talk. My husband is forever amazed at how much time my friends and I can spend in conversation.

If you're like me, you've probably come to realize the truth of this verse from Proverbs, "Where talk is plentiful, sin is not wanting." Somehow, the more we say, the more occasions there are to offend in the area of speech. Because a well-guarded tongue is so crucial to our Christian witness, I've reflected on what we can do to tame our tongues. The following are some points I've gleaned from the Scripture that I'm working on. Perhaps they may help you.

Believe in the Transforming Power of The Holy Spirit. Years ago, I invited a former drug addict from Teen Challenge to speak to my high school students about Christ. After the first class it was clear the speaker needed a microphone because she was so soft-spoken. The woman shook her head in amusement. "I had one of the loudest, coarsest mouths you can imagine. The fact that these girls can't hear me without a microphone gives testimony to the transforming power of the Holy Spirit." What the Spirit has done for her, He can do for us as well. If we turn to the Lord, admitting our need for help in using our tongues rightly, He will not fail us. Repentance and faith always unleash the transforming power of the Holy Spirit in our lives.

Daily Prayer and Scripture Reading. We must present ourselves to the Lord, submit to Him, and grow in union with Him. This doesn't mean we won't fall through our words, perhaps many times a day. But when we're growing in union with the Lord, at least we know we're falling. Without prayer, we might not even realize our shortcomings in the area of speech. The more we pray and read His word, the more we're attuned to the convicting power of the Holy Spirit. We can identify speech patterns that need to change.

Get familiar with the teaching of Scripture on proper use of the tongue. One of my dear friends made a file of index cards with individual quotes from Scripture concerning speech. Each day she placed a new quote on the windowsill above her sink. While at work she meditated on God's word. "Say nothing harmful small or great" (Sirach 6:1) is one I remember seeing there. No wonder her speech is so gracious!

Guard Your Minds and Hearts. St. Paul says, "Take every thought captive to Christ" (II Corinthians 10:5). What comes out of our mouths has first been born in our hearts and pondered in our minds before it's expressed. Learn to nip those critical, unloving, sinful thoughts in the bud before they go from your heart into your mind and out of your lips.

Make a Commitment to Positive Speech. Years ago my husband and I agreed to compliment each other at least once a day. At first it was awkward and we'd joke about saying three positive things on Wednesday so we'd be caught up on compliments until the weekend! But after the initial embarrassment, we both began to see the good fruit in our lives. Now positive speech about each other is so natural, we need few reminders. Look for opportunities to say good things to one another on birthdays, anniversaries, and holidays. Make a commitment to it, and I guarantee you'll see results.

Never Repeat Gossip. Don't even repeat "charismatic gossip."

Do you know what that is? The phone rings and you say, "Now, don't tell this to anybody. I wouldn't even share this with you except for prayer, but did you hear about…" Much gossip can be cloaked in prayer requests. We need to examine our hearts before the Lord. In Sirach we read, "Let anything you hear die within you. Be assured, it will not make you burst. When a fool hears something, he is in labor, like a woman giving birth to a child" (Sirach 19:9-10). Let's learn to let certain things die within us.

Replace Grumbling with Gratitude. "Dedicate yourselves to thankfulness" (Colossians 3:15). That implies a firm decision to give thanks always and for everything. Here's one I need to work on continually. When our water faucet broke I left my husband a note which read, "Faucet broken. In everything give thanks!" We need to encourage one another in our families and communities to give thanks instead of gripe.

Say Only What Helps. In Ephesians 4:29-30 we read, "Never let evil talk pass from your lips. Say only the good things men need to hear, things that will really help them. Do nothing to sadden the Holy Spirit with whom you were sealed against the day of redemption." One night I walked into our prayer meeting, and in the course of a conversation I said something which, while true, was totally unnecessary. It put a certain group of people in a bad light. By the time I walked up to my seat, I knew that I had saddened the Holy Spirit. I apologized to the Lord and to my friends. What I said didn't really help. So ask yourself, "Will this really help?" If not, don't say it.

Make a Regular Examination of Conscience about Speech. Am I using my tongue to glorify God and to build up my brothers and sisters, especially those who are closest to me? Or am I using my tongue to worship the Lord in one breath and in the next to injure the Body of Christ?

I pray that the following verse from Proverbs 31 may take on flesh in me as I yield to the transforming power of the Holy Spirit. "The teaching of kindness is on her tongue." May this be true in your life as well.

Where Are Your Eyes?

My friend sounded anxious. A routine check up at the doctor's office uncovered a suspicious growth. You know what follows. X-rays, hospitalization, biopsies, tests and maybe the worst. It's easy to give in to the fear that tightens its grip around our hearts when we receive such news about ourselves or a loved one. But Jesus speaks His word to us today as surely as He spoke it to the parents of the dying child long ago. "Fear is useless. What is needed is trust (Luke 8:50)." Trust. Followers of Jesus don't have to yield to fear as we face the future, no matter what awaits us. He loves us and we can trust Him.

I was talking to Babsie Bleasdell of Trinidad and I mentioned my friend's impending surgery. Babsie, who always had a word of truth, gave me this prophetic exhortation to share with my friend. She said, "Let your eyes be on Jesus alone. Do not let your eyes fall to this lump. Let your eyes be on Him. Let His eyes be on the lump. There can be no ifs, ands or buts about it! Your eyes on Him. His eyes on the problem." In other words, don't make any excuses about why you have a right to worry. Look at Jesus. Trust Him. He'll take care of you. That word of the Lord through Babsie brought peace and confidence into my friend's heart and mine as well. Our eyes on Him. His eyes on our circumstances.

It reminds me of the gospel story about St. Peter walking on the water. As long as St. Peter kept his eyes fixed firmly on Jesus, he could pass over the sea barefoot. The impossible became possible as Peter obeyed the word of Jesus, "Come!" But as soon as Peter took his eyes off of the Lord Jesus, as soon as his eyes fell to the sea beneath him, he began to sink. Isn't it easy to identify with our beloved St. Peter who started out in confidence and faith but ended up overwhelmed by the water? Without trust he sank.

Within this past year the Lord has been hammering home to me the importance of trust in my relationship to Him. I was having health problems that were causing me fear and anxiety, so I turned to Jesus in prayer. In the depths of my heart the Lord seemed to say, "Your health is My concern." It's as if He had to remind me that I do not belong to myself. I belong to Him. Everything about my life concerns Him. It's almost too good to be true! The great God of the universe chooses to be concerned about me—and you—and every other living person.

Then He helped me identify an everyday example of the kind of trust He expects from me. Some years ago my husband Al told me not to worry about putting gas in our mini-van. "I'll take care of it for you." he said. And that was it! Even though I'm the primary driver of the van all week long, never once since then have I put gas in it. In fact, I never even look at the gas gauge anymore! I simply trust that Al will be true to his word. I don't need to check up on him. I don't need to worry. Al is trustworthy and he will do exactly what he says. But as wonderful as my husband is, he's only a man. If I can trust another human being to keep his word, why can't I accord the same confident trust to the Lord Jesus Christ who died and rose for me?

Think about it. When we get on board a plane, we don't require the pilot to show us his license. We trust. When we go to a restaurant we don't phone ahead to be sure they have food. We trust. Jesus desires and deserves our confident trust that He will care for us in all our needs. That is, if only we keep our eyes on Him and never let them fall.

Where are your eyes today? On your bank account? On your son, your daughter? On your health problems? Or are they on Jesus? Turn your eyes to Him. Make no excuse. Don't check the gas gauge. Be like David who said, *"I kept the Lord before me always. With Him on my right hand I shall never be moved"* (Psalm 16:8).

Twenty Years Later

An invitation to my high school reunion arrived in the mail recently. Can it be possible that twenty years have passed so quickly? A glance in the mirror at my sprinkling of grey hair confirmed the truth: time has gone by. Although unable to attend the reunion, I was eager for news about old friends. Fortunately, the reunion committee prepared a booklet with information about the class. How interesting to read the whereabouts of friends from Irvington High. Such a booklet cannot, however, contain the many joys and sorrows, successes, failures and unexpected circumstances that have come our way. My own life is certainly different than I would have ever imagined back then.

The reunion caused me to reflect on the basic change that has taken place for me over these twenty years. At the time of my graduation from high school, my main goal was to be successful. Like most young people, I thought that achieving success, with the accompanying prestige and financial rewards, was the most important thing in life. I knew the Lord in some way, but my basic relationship to Him was one of asking Him to bless my plans and grant my desires.

Here I stand, twenty years later, knowing clearly that neither fame nor fortune, power nor prestige can bring lasting happiness. The incomparable grace of God has touched my life in the Baptism in the Holy Spirit to convince me that knowing, loving and serving Jesus is the only thing that really matters. Doing the Father's will and not our own is the key to true peace and security for the future. Even our difficulties are transformed when we love the Lord because they provide opportunities to grow in holiness.

But I'm not the only member of my class that has come to this discovery. After the reunion I received a beautiful letter from a classmate describing her conversion to Christ. An even more dramatic change has taken place in her life than in mine because, you see, my friend, Cindi, is Jewish.

During her childhood she was taught about Jewish holidays but not about God's personal love. After marrying a Catholic and starting a family, Cindi was gradually drawn to faith in Christ and was baptized. Now she writes, "Every day of my life seems to be a closer walk with our Lord. He has made a new person out of me, giving me confidence, strength and courage."

Within the past year, my friend received the Baptism in the Holy Spirit and is full of zeal to spread the Good News. She said she grieves for "sleeping Catholics" who don't realize the great gift they have received in the friendship of Christ. Her husband teases about his Jewish wife who became a Catholic Charismatic and now brings him to Church! What a miracle of God's grace!

Knowing Jesus as a personal friend, Savior and Lord has transformed Cindi's life and it's transformed mine. I pray it may transform your life as well. No matter what changes the next twenty years may bring, "I believe nothing can happen that will outweigh the supreme advantage of knowing Christ Jesus my Lord." (Philippians 3:8).

Hangers

"There are never enough when you need them!", I muttered while in the laundry room on a frantic search for hangers. The buzzer from the dryer had already sounded and unless I found more hangers soon, the clothes would be wrinkled. Perish the thought of having to iron them!

On my next round of errands I planned to buy hangers, but when I found out how much they cost, I decided to shop around later for a better price. I was pressed for time right then because of preparations for an out-of-town trip.

The next weekend my husband, Al, and I flew to Texas to speak on the topic of marriage and family life. We had been praying over Bible passages on marriage and rereading the best books on family life. We wanted to present a Scriptural understanding of the marriage relationship with special emphasis on the importance of love and good communication. Because we thought people would have questions about the text in Ephesians 5:21-33 concerning order in the marriage relationship, we wanted to address that as well. Little did I realize that my own understanding of Ephesians 5 was about to be deepened—and not because of my careful talk preparations either.

While we were in Texas, all was peaceful in our own relationship until it was time to leave the motel. I noticed that my husband had closed the suitcase without packing the four hangers on which we carried our clothes.

"Open the suitcase and put these hangers in for me," I asked him hurriedly. Our hosts were knocking at the door. It was time to leave.

"No, let's leave them," my husband responded. "They're only hangers and the suitcase was hard to close. We don't want to be late."

My reaction was immediate. I picked up the four hangers, clutched them under my arm defiantly and in no uncertain terms announced, "If I have to carry these hangers back to New Orleans under my arm, they're going with me! I need more hangers right now. Do you know how much they cost? I will not leave these hangers behind!"

There was another knock at the door but I wasn't budging without my hangers. Without a word, Al opened the suitcase and put the hangers in, but it was clear he was angry. In an icy silence we headed off to tell other couples how to get along with each other. What irony!

As soon as we walked out of the room, the Holy Spirit convicted me. I knew I was wrong to insist on my own way. Those four hangers certainly weren't worth putting a strain on our relationship. I could have expressed my opinion without turning the situation into a confrontation. After all, he didn't know I needed hangers. A gentler tone of voice, a more reasonable attitude would have helped. In short, I lacked a cooperative spirit. I had gained my four precious hangers but lost my peace. Before we gave our talks I whispered an apology to my husband. Although he forgave me, we were under a strain for the rest of the day.

Of course, St. Paul doesn't only speak to wives in the Ephesians passage but to husbands as well when he exhorts them to love their wives and lay down their lives for them. My husband realized this. The week after our trip I noticed a stack of empty hangers in each of my closets. Do you know where they came from? Al! Upon returning home, my husband made a thorough search of each closet to collect empty hangers since I let him know how much they meant to me. Now that's love!

And as if I hadn't learned my lesson, the next day a friend dropped by to lend me some clothes. She knew nothing about the hangers story. Liz said she was planning to carry the clothes in a paper bag, but the Lord prompted her otherwise. "Hang the clothes on hangers for Patti. She may need extra hangers!" I'm convinced the Lord has a sense of humor!

Through seemingly small incidents the Holy Spirit is often waiting to teach us great truths. That passage in Ephesians 5 states, "Defer to one another out of reverence for Christ. Each one should love his wife as he loves himself, the wife for her part showing respect for her husband" (Ephesians 5:21-33). I can never again look at a hanger without being reminded of my lesson on marriage. Defer to one another. Love one another. Respect one another. Be at peace.

All I Want for Christmas

Do you remember the song, "All I want for Christmas is my two front teeth?" With toothless precision every December some little child sang, "Yeth, all I want for Chrithmath ith my two front teeth, tho I can with you Merry Chrithmath!"

That song, secular though it is, speaks to me in a special way about the mystery of the Incarnation. Our heavenly Father chose to reveal His love for us in the God-man Jesus Christ. There is absolutely no aspect of our human lives that is unimportant to Him. Jesus not only sympathizes with our weakness (see Hebrews 4:15), He knows firsthand what it is to live this earthly life. He too was once a young child unable to pronounce certain sounds because His front teeth were missing. Imagine that! And He still concerns Himself with front teeth. Just ask Peter and Becky.

When my son, Peter, was a toddler he fell and hit his mouth. One front tooth blackened and had to be extracted. When the two permanent teeth came in they were healthy, but badly spotted. This was a source of real embarrassment for my son. You know how school children can tease. "What's the matter, Peter? Didn't you brush your teeth?", some would jibe. Even though Peter is well-adjusted, confident and popular, those two front teeth were holding him back. He wasn't smiling readily for fear of ridicule.

During a regular dental check-up last December I asked the dentist how costly it would be to bond enamel to those badly stained front teeth. Instead of quoting a price the dentist turned to Peter with a question.

"When's your birthday?"

Peter replied it had just passed.

"Well, I've got a birthday present for you, Peter. I'm making those two teeth white as a gift!"

Can you imagine Peter's joy? The dentist was not a personal friend, so his generosity came as a real surprise. Peter returned home grinning from ear to ear to display his gorgeous white teeth and he hasn't stopped smiling since! Last Christmas will always be remembered in the Mansfield family as the year Peter got two new front teeth as a birthday gift.

Now for Becky's story. Her mom, Brenda, inherited a rare dental problem from her mother. Brenda was missing her two permanent front teeth. As a child she suffered pain and embarrassment. As an adult she worried constantly that this condition might be passed along to her daughter, Becky. Brenda often prayed for a normal set of permanent teeth for her child.

But when Becky was eight, the x-rays confirmed Brenda's worst fears. Becky's two permanent front teeth were missing. Brenda was devastated, but she didn't stop praying. In fact, she prayed with greater fervor, asking Jesus to supply the two front teeth despite the doctor's report.

Becky had her first orthodontist appointment a few weeks later. Another set of x-rays were taken and to the doctor's amazement, Becky's teeth, *all of them*, were there! He compared the two x-rays and said "The teeth weren't there two weeks ago, now they are! I just can't explain it." Ask Becky if Jesus cares about her smile.

Two front teeth—insignificant to God? Never! Jesus, the

babe of Bethlehem, the child of Nazareth, the man of Galilee knows and cares about everything. As Lord and Master of all, He concerns Himself with the smallest details of our lives.

Your trust in Jesus' love honors Him. Don't hesitate to bring your every need to Jesus with confidence. Remember Peter. Remember Becky. All they wanted for Christmas was their two front teeth so they could wish you a Merry Christmas!

If You Love Me

Money. Sex. Children. Work. In-laws. Faith. Did you discuss these topics during your engagement? We did. In our Pre-Cana course we were encouraged to communicate about all of the areas that would deeply affect our married lives. The discussions were not meant to prove one of us right and the other one wrong. We were simply trying to understand each other's thoughts.

I remember a conversation my fiancé and I had about faith. He had asked me the following question: "What do you think is at the heart of the Gospel? If you had to put it in a word, what would it be?" My answer was immediate: "Love!" After all, doesn't everyone know that? I felt that the Gospel could best be summed up as a relationship of love between God and His people, manifested in Jesus Christ our Lord and Savior.

Then I proceeded to quote several Scripture passages to illustrate my point (and to impress my fiancé who majored in theology). "Yes, God so loved the world that He gave His only Son, that whoever believes in Him may not die but have eternal life" (John 3:16). That passage has even been called "the gospel in miniature." I reminded him of the well-known passage from Chapter 13 of First Corinthians: "There are in the end three things that last: faith, hope, and love, and the greatest of these is love." And. Of course, St. John makes it clear that love is at the heart of our faith when he says quite simply, "God is love" (I John 4:16).

I fully expected my fiancé to congratulate me on my insight, but instead he remained silent. I began to suspect he had a different opinion.

As we talked about it, he said that he felt the gospel could best be expressed by the word "obedience." Naturally, he had his own share of Scripture quotations to confirm this. His favorite passage is from Psalm 40:9 where David said, "To do Your will, O my God, is my delight, and Your law is within my heart!" Then he reminded me of Mary's response of faith which was so precious to God. "I am the servant of the Lord. Let it be done to me as you say" (Luke 1:38). And Jesus Himself expressed His relationship to God in terms of obedience, "I always do what pleases my Father" (John 8:29).

Although I wanted to argue that I was right and my fiancé was wrong, I couldn't. Each of us had grasped something of the truth. Love and obedience are like two sides of the same coin. Love without obedience can be little more than an empty show of emotion. But obedience without love seems more characteristic of a hired servant, not a devoted child.

I couldn't help but think about the connection between love and obedience while Catholics in the United States prepared for the visit of Pope Saint John Paul II in 1987. When he came to the States in 1979, I eagerly watched the news coverage. The display of affection from the young people in Washington, D.C., was especially moving. Do you remember their placards and chants? "John Paul II, we love you!" Over and over again they shouted out their love for the Holy Father. As I listened to their enthusiastic cheers I found myself hoping that their love would last. I wondered what influences would shape the lives of these young Catholics after the Pope returned to Rome. Would it be the standard of Christ and His Church or the standard of the world that would guide them?

The words of Jesus from John's Gospel came home to me with greater force than ever. "Anyone who loves Me will be true to My word (John 14:23). "He who obeys the commandments he has from Me is the man who loves Me" (John 14:21). To put it another way, "If you love Me, listen to My teaching. If you love Me, pay attention to what I say. If you really love Me, let My words form you." It's not enough to say that we love the Vicar of Christ. Our love must be accompanied by a spirit of obedience in order to be complete.

 **Seasons**

Moving from the North to the Deep South has been quite an experience. I remember that summer day I arrived in New Orleans, July 4, 1971, and was greeted, "Welcome to N'Awlins on the fourth of Jooolie! How was all ya'll's trip?" Could this still be English, I wondered? A Southern friend had already teased me about changing my name to Patti Sue or Patti Jo. To my horror, I spotted a huge roach in the apartment where I was staying. One of the girls referred to it as a "friendly little critter!" Between the strange accents, stifling heat and awful insects, I thought I'd soon be heading back North!

By now, almost twenty years later, I feel at home in the South and even spice up my speech with an occasional "Ya'll come." It's only in the Fall when I really miss the North. Autumn was always my favorite season with cool breezes, gorgeous foliage, plaid dresses and a new school year. Living in the North, I learned to appreciate and welcome the distinctive beauty of each season. That's impossible here when it's 80 degrees at Christmastime.

I've often reflected that there are seasons in our spiritual lives as well. The Lord wants to teach us how to seek Him consistently through the changes each season brings. In my own prayer life I've certainly experienced seasonal changes.

Like so many, when I was first baptized in the Spirit, I developed a desire for prayer. I longed to commune with God and at first it was easy and consoling to pray. As a student I could arrange my schedule to include daily Mass and time before the Blessed Sacrament. Weekly prayer meetings nourished me, as well as daily prayer sessions in the dorm.

This was a beautiful season in my life, full of all the freshness and wonder of new-found love. It was springtime. During this season God taught me the importance of daily prayer, Scripture reading and a sacramental life. I came to appreciate Christian community and I learned that prayer must overflow into service.

As a single working woman, I was still able to spend several hours a day before the Blessed Sacrament. I remember feeling almost guilty because of these wonderful opportunities for quiet prayer. Then one day the Lord seemed to say, "Enjoy this now, because you won't always have it. Learn to pray wherever you are." How right He was!

Once I became a wife and mother, my time was never my own. As much as I desired to spend uninterrupted hours of prayer, they were impossible to plan. This season, like summertime, has required me to be more creative. I've learned to seize time for prayer while the baby is napping, during a late night feeding, waiting for the doctor, under the hairdryer, at a ball game.

The Lord says, "When you call Me, when you go to pray to Me, I will listen to you. When you look for Me, you will find Me" (Jeremiah 29:12). True to His promise, the Lord always meets us wherever we are if we turn to Him. One mother of eleven told me that when her children were little, she would retreat to the bathroom for 10 minutes of quiet prayer. At least in there they would leave her alone!

Of course, sometimes we excuse ourselves from prayer because of family or work and we're not being honest. If we examine our situation more closely we'll see that sin, fear, lack of faith and laziness are often the real reasons we don't pray. Daily choices reveal our true priorities. Do I pray now or phone a friend? Do I pray now or read the paper? Do I pray now or take a nap? Do I pray now or watch a football game? Certainly we all need to cultivate friendships, stay informed, rest and recreate. But if Jesus is really first in our hearts, our greatest need is to come to know and love Him in prayer, no matter what the season. Longing for God must permeate our lives summer, spring, winter and fall.

Years ago I saw a little girl skipping on the steps of the altar after Mass. She seemed so happy playing in her Father's house. After she left, the church door opened again and I heard her say in a very loud whisper, "Jesus, I want to come back and be with You forever and ever!" Just a little girl in the springtime of life, and yet she already had such a great longing for God.

May that same desire and longing for God fill each of our lives and bring us to prayer from season to season, until one day we see Him face to face.

Master at Work

Just a few months ago my husband and I were invited to attend a session of the Christian Oilmen's Conference in New Orleans. I was eager to go when I found out that Rev. Harald Bredesen was a speaker. It had been more than twenty years since last we met, yet when I approached Rev. Bredesen he immediately called me by name. How amazing! This marvelous man of God has an exceptional gift for communicating the love of the Lord and the excitement of serving Him. Our reunion flooded me with memories.

In March of 1967, Pastor Bredesen came to visit our Catholic prayer group at Duquesne, recently formed when we experienced the Baptism in the Spirit. At the time I was puzzling over some personal questions including a decision about whether to pursue a summer trip to France. It seemed that as Harald Bredesen spoke many of my questions were answered. He shared a dream he had of bringing some of us Spirit-filled young Catholics to his Dutch Reformed Church in Mt. Vernon, New York. There he hoped we could share in Christian fellowship and witness to young people about Jesus. A friend seated next to me nudged my elbow and whispered, "That's for you, Patti!" After some prayer and reflection, I canceled my studies in France and decided to dedicate my life to the work of evangelization.

Nine of us from Duquesne moved to Mt. Vernon that summer in fulfillment of Pastor Bredesen's dream. It was like enrolling in a "Holy Spirit School" just to be around him! Every day was filled with amazing Holy Spirit happenings. We saw

God provide for our material needs. For example, our first grocery bill of $60 was paid from Rev. Bredesen's pocket. That night someone handed him three $20 bills "to help with the Catholic kids!"

Christian love was action, not mere words, in the Bredesen household as they graciously moved their entire family into one bedroom to make room for us. We learned about Christian unity as we shared time of morning prayer. These dear people even adjusted their style of praying if it made us uncomfortable. In every way we were welcomed and honored as their guests.

My most significant lessons came as I watched Pastor Bredesen minister to young people in the streets of Mt. Vernon. I had read about street evangelism in *The Cross and the Switchblade*. Here I saw a master at work!

Following Pastor Bredesen's example, we learned how to follow the Holy Spirit's lead in proclaiming the Good News. One day after witnessing to some teenage boys, my friend and I tried to speak to their girlfriends. The boys whisked the girls off in a car, and we were left standing on the sidewalk.

"What would Pastor Bredesen do?" we asked ourselves. Immediately we knew the answer. Heads bowed in prayer, we said, "Jesus, if You want these girls to be evangelized, send them back." Within moments the car returned, and the boys called out, "Okay. We've heard your story, but they haven't. Tell them." Alleluia! The girls were Jewish.

The weeks I spent with Harald Bredesen left a lasting impression on my life. His lesson was clear: The Holy Spirit is in charge. It's worth sacrificing everything to be faithful to His lead. In the thrilling book *Yes, Lord*, Pastor Bredesen shares about how costly that faithfulness can he. It's clear to me how significant this man has been to God's plan for the church in this century. It was a lonely road to travel when God led Harald Bredesen, a Lutheran, into the Baptism in the Spirit in 1946. He was among the first to witness and foster the modern day outpouring of the Spirit among the mainline churches. In 1959 God told Pastor Bredesen to "hold nothing back." He shared his experience concerning the Baptism in the Spirit with Norman Vincent Peale and Peale's wife. Through them, *Guideposts'* senior editor, John Sherrill, was baptized in the Spirit. Sherrill in turn "held nothing back." He was writing *They Speak With Other Tongues* when Harald Bredesen introduced him to a street preacher named David Wilkerson. Together Sherrill and Wilkerson wrote *The Cross and the Switchblade.*

These two books were read by some Duquesne professors in 1966 and were instrumental in bringing the Baptism in the Spirit into the Catholic Church. Harald Bredesen was a key person in all these events. He has been used mightily to minister to world leaders ever since.

How grateful I am that one man had the courage to say, "Yes, Lord." In 1989 Rev. Bredesen received an Honorary Doctorate from Franciscan University in Steubenville in virtue of his courageous ecumenism and faithfulness to the Holy Spirit.

Reverend Bredesen, we Catholics thank you, we honor you, and we love you!

 **Beauty Secrets**

At the end of John's Gospel we read that if all the works of the Lord Jesus were written the world itself could not contain the books! I was reminded of this recently after our annual Holy Spirit Women's Retreat as each woman shared what Jesus had done for her. Here's just a sampling.

> *"I went on a diet during retreat, because I shed 20 pounds of guilt!"*

> *"I've been so loved I feel like a queen!"*

> *"My knee injury was healed as I looked at Jesus in the Blessed Sacrament."*

> *"I'm more in love with Jesus than ever!"*

> *"I feel called to intercede for the needs of the Church."*

> *"My mother and daughter have been exuding love ever since they were baptized in the Spirit. Now I understand their joy."*

While listening to the testimonies, I marveled at the radiant beauty of these women who had been with Jesus. The theme for our retreat was, "Come to the Water." Each woman, like the woman at the well, had encountered the merciful Master who gave her living water, then sent her back to town proclaiming His name. We returned with a sense of our dignity as women, loved by God, empowered for service, as daughters of the Church.

What a difference from the women's retreat my friend attended elsewhere. The person giving the talks said she wanted to "woo the women into a new consciousness—to recognize the goddess within." Then she proceeded to criticize the Church, its teaching and practices, with a special disdain for those in authority.

My friend went on her retreat expecting to be refreshed by living water; she came home grieving over polluted water instead. How heartbreaking that many of the women present didn't even realize that the retreat director was speaking her own mind, not the mind of the Church.

Pay attention, my friends! "This is not a time for believing everyone. Believe only those you see modeling their lives on the life of Christ." So said St. Teresa of Avila, a woman worth listening to.

In fact, I've recently been reading St. Teresa of Avila and St. Catherine of Siena, both Doctors of the Church, to discover the source of their holiness as women. I feel like one woman asking another woman to share her secret for radiant beauty. I'm saying, "How can I get to look like you?"

Do you know what I found in them? An immense longing for God! An overwhelming experience of His merciful love! A tremendous desire for the salvation of souls! By wholehearted surrender to the Lord, constant, humble prayer and obedience to the Father's will, these women profoundly affected not only the Church of their times but all generations to come. Because they had influence with God in prayer, they had influence with others in word and deed.

But for me, the most thrilling discovery I've made in my reading is really quite simple. It is this: *the Jesus Catherine knew, the Jesus Teresa knew, is my Jesus! He is your Jesus! He is "Jesus Christ, the same yesterday, today and forever"*

(Hebrews 13:8). In Christ and through His blood, you and I have the same access to the throne of God as did Catherine, Teresa and all God's holy ones! There is much talk about influence and power among women in today's Church. *Access to God! That's influence! Access to God! That's power!*

My sisters, do you realize that we have freedom of access to the very throne of God? As we position ourselves there, before Him, we will discover incredible influence and power. God has a work for us to do in the rebuilding of His Church. But we must be emptied of our own ideas, in order to understand His.

You see, nothing external can keep us from the Lord and a wholehearted surrender to His will. My sisters on our Holy Spirit Retreat realized this. No spouse, child or community member, no job, position or lack of one, no sickness nor any other circumstance can limit our access to God in Christ. However, what can limit us is internal—pride, unforgiveness, resentment, hatred, selfishness, envy, misplaced priorities—in short, sin.

As I ponder the lives of St. Catherine and St. Teresa of long ago, as I admire women like Blessed Mother Teresa and Sr. Briege of today, I see women who have first found their influence with God in prayer. Then, obedient to the particular call they received, as loyal daughters of the Church, they've accomplished great works in the Church.

Notice the sequence: *Access. Surrender. Obedience.* And then a radiant beauty, a radiant love that gives a Christian woman undisputed influence and power to draw others to God.

That's the way of Mary, our Blessed Mother, the way of St. Catherine, St. Teresa, and all the great women saints. That's the model I want to follow, the kind of woman I want to be. What about you?

The Father's Hand

As a child growing up in New Jersey, just 40 minutes outside of New York City, I used to eagerly anticipate visits to the city for cultural events in the company of my father. I never learned my own way around Manhattan. I simply held my father's hand. I didn't have to know the way. He did. And that was security enough for me.

On Tuesday, September 11, 2001, I watched with horror as this beloved city was devastated by the collapse of the World Trade Center Towers. I wondered if my own loved ones in the New York City area were safe. Thank God, they were. But there are thousands, not only from America, but citizens of the entire world, who lost their lives in that terrorist attack and the other related crashes and attacks.

"Where sin abounds, grace abounds still more," the Scriptures tell us (Romans 5:20). And it is true. In the midst of such unbridled evil, God's love has been poured out upon America. Grace is here and self-giving is the response. One woman who escaped the World Trade Center tearfully described the streams of young firemen who were rushing into the burning building, laying down their lives that others might be saved. Another survivor described a moving aspect of the escape: men assisting women, women helping each other, the strong carrying the weak. New York City could no longer be criticized for its rudeness and impatience. It is a city where heroes live and have died. There was a Franciscan priest, chaplain for the firefighters, who died while administering the last rites to a victim. The scene of rescue workers carrying his limp body away from the rubble is but one of many modern day "Stations of the Cross."

In an amazing television interview two days after the attack, Franklin Graham (son of the famous evangelist Billy Graham), did not try to explain the mystery of iniquity. But he seized the moment and in prime time proclaimed the Good News that "God so loved the world that He gave His only Son, that whoever believes in Him should not perish but have eternal life (John 3:16)." Mr. Graham was loving but unyielding in his urgency. Now is the time to get right with God.

"Unless you repent you will all likewise perish" (Luke 13:1-5). Jesus addressed these searing words to those who told him about the people who were killed in the fall of the tower in Siloam. Within hours of the attack on our country, my husband was reminded of this very passage of Scripture. We see in it a call to ourselves first of all, to our country and to the world. *Repent. Turn back to God. Pray and make peace.* And it is our choice (a favorite word in my country)—a choice which will determine whether we will live in fear or live in faith—faith in the Son of God who loved us and gave Himself for us (cf. Galatians 2:20).

I am reminded of a great woman of God, Corrie ten Boom, who lived through the dark days of World War II. When she confided to her father the fears she had about the future, wondering whether she would have the courage to endure all that was to come, he asked her this question. "Corrie, when do I give you your train ticket, months before you travel or just as you are boarding the train?" She answered, "Father, you give it to me at the moment I need it." At the moment we need it, God will supply.

"Be not afraid!" How much I have been pondering the immensity of these words of Jesus, reiterated by the Holy Father as we approached the millennium. In his apostolic letter, *Novo Millennio Ineunte*, 35, Pope Saint John Paul II wrote, "We do not know what the new millennium has in store for us, but we are certain that it is safe in the hands of Christ, the King of kings and Lord of lords (Revelation 19:16)...." Safe in His hands—just like I was safe in the hands of my father as we walked the streets of New York City so many years ago. My hand was in his, though I did not know the way. His hand was my security. Let us pray that we all may clasp with faith the hand of our loving Father for He is worthy of our trust.

This column was written for an Italian Catholic Charismatic Renewal magazine just after 9/11.

 First Love

"There are so few who really love Me, even among those consecrated to Me."

I sensed the Lord speaking these words to me many years ago while I was praying in a little church in Old Tappan, New York. I was startled.

"So few?" I wondered. "Does the Lord really have so few who love Him?" Then I read in the Autobiography of St. Margaret Mary that the Lord had also complained to her of the same thing. Very few souls really love Him. As He revealed to her the depths of love in His Sacred Heart, He said something like this: "Behold this Heart which so loves men and is so little loved in return."

I've begun to understand that the Heart of Jesus is human as well as divine. And Jesus not only loves us, but He longs for our love in return. It matters to Him how we respond. He rejoices in our sincere devotion and is saddened when our hearts grow cold. He is, in a sense, starved for His people to express their love for Him.

Remember in Revelation 2 where the Lord says to the church in Ephesus, "But I have this against you, that you have abandoned the love you had at first." And to the church in Laodicea the Lord says, "Would that you were cold or hot! So because you are lukewarm, and neither cold nor hot, I will spew you out of My mouth" (Revelation 3:15-16).

Surely our devotion to the Lord must involve more than mere words or outward signs of reverence. We need to love and serve one another. We need to do the spiritual and corporal works of mercy. And yet our visible expressions of love and honor of Jesus are some indication of our spiritual fervor. How can we honor Him? Several things come readily to mind.

When I was a child we were taught to show reverence for the Lord by wearing our "Sunday best" for church. Our family was of modest means, yet we always wore dress clothes when we went to Mass. It was a mark of respect for the Lord and the Lord's Day. This simple means of honoring the Lord seems to have been forgotten as adults, teens and children come to Sunday Mass in T-shirts and shorts.

"Worship the Lord in holy attire" wrote King David in Psalm 96:9. True, it takes more of an effort to dress up for church. But by making that effort we're showing that we love and respect the great King of Kings present in the Blessed Sacrament. If we dress for a social event, we can surely dress for worship.

Do you remember as a youngster that you bowed your head at the name of Jesus? I do. When I was first taught to do this I was very conscientious about it. Over the years I fell out of the habit, along with most Catholics of the church. But as I've come to realize in prayer, how deeply our Lord longs to be loved, reverenced and honored, I've begun to bow my head once more when I hear His holy name. One of my favorite songs is this hymn from the Divine Office:

> At the name of Jesus, every knee must bow,
> Every tongue confess Him King of Glory now.
> 'Tis the Father's pleasure we should call Him Lord
> Who from the beginning was the mighty Word.

Our entire bodies can be used to reverence the Lord who died and rose for our sake. Bending the knee, bowing the head, humbling the heart are all expressions of love. Let's do them again willingly and gladly. He is worthy!

As we show reverence for God and the things of God, we'll become more sensitive to the myriad ways the Lord is being offended in our world. My teenage son tells me how rough the language can be in high school. He hears the Lord's name taken in vain every day. "What should I do?" he asked me. I used this as an opportunity to teach him about reparation.

"Son, when I hear someone profaning the name of Jesus I pray silently telling the Lord I love Him and asking forgiveness for the person who is cursing. It's a way of making up to the Lord for the offense." I had an experience of this just recently.

I was waiting in line at a pharmacy check-out counter when a young man behind me began to profane the name of Jesus. Inwardly I winced, but began to pray, asking forgiveness for this man and telling Jesus I love His name. I really wanted to reach out to this poor fellow and lift him out of his pit of profanity. Correcting him would have accomplished nothing. Instead, the Holy Spirit seemed to lead me to make conversation with him on a superficial level. I didn't speak to him about the Lord directly, but the desire in my heart was to share the goodness and love of Jesus with him. As we conversed he seemed to soften. After my purchase he smiled at me and said, "Have a good day now!"

I'd like to believe that my prayer and simple kindness helped lift him up and transform his cursing to a blessing. May he too come to know Jesus fully one day and reverence His holy name!

Once as a penance my spiritual director, Father Andrew, told me to ask for the grace of a warm heart. I didn't understand at first what that meant. But as I pondered it, I realized that a warm heart is the opposite of a cold heart. Warm hearts want to reverence, honor and love Jesus. Warm hearts are fired by the Holy Spirit. Warm hearts never abandon the devotion of that first love. Warm hearts are sensitive to the needs of others.

Let's all pray for the grace of a warm heart—a heart to love the Lord Jesus as He desires and deserves to be loved.

 Two-Edged Sword

"Indeed, God's word is living and effective, sharper than any two-edged sword. It penetrates and divides soul and spirit, joints and marrow. It judges the reflections and thoughts of the heart. Nothing is concealed from Him. All lies bare and exposed to the eyes of Him to whom we must render an account" (Hebrews 4:12-13).

God's word is alive! That fact is a source of great joy and consolation, but it is also a source of constant challenge and conviction as we follow Jesus. I was amazed after receiving the Baptism in the Holy Spirit to find out how alive God's word could be. The words of Scripture seemed to leap off the page to speak to my heart. In Psalm 119 we read that a young person can keep his life pure by guarding it according to God's word. God's word needs to be stored up in our hearts that we might not sin against the Lord. As the Holy Spirit teaches us, He often uses the Scripture which we have read and meditated upon to shed light on the circumstances of our everyday life.

I had a powerful experience years ago of this "two-edged sword" of God's word piercing my thoughts. I was visiting my family, and as I unpacked I noticed that my brother was using a cheaper brand of contact lens solution than the one which I brought home. This meant very little until the next morning when I noticed my bottle of solution left open on the sink. Obviously my brother had tried it out. I used the solution myself and put it on the shelf.

The next morning once again, I found the bottle open on the sink. I was a little irritated but I used the solution and returned it to the shelf. When on the third day I found my contact lens solution had been used, I was upset! There it was, left open day after day, evaporating into thin air! I took the bottle and hid it in my room. After all, I had invested in a better brand of contact lens solution and I should benefit from it, right?

Later that day at Mass, during the Offertory, I said to the Lord, "I offer you everything I am and everything I have." There immediately came to mind a vivid picture of my bottle of contact lens solution with a Scripture passage underneath. The passage, from Luke's Gospel, concerns someone who wants Jesus to settle a dispute over an inheritance. Jesus says, "Avoid greed in all its forms, for a man's life does not consist in the abundance of his possessions" (Luke 12:15).

God's living word had penetrated my thoughts and revealed my actions for what they were: selfishness. I knew I could not honestly offer myself to the Lord without giving Him this "precious" bottle of contact lens solution. I became determined to remove it from hiding so my brother could use it again. Perhaps this seems like a small incident, but many relationships and families have been destroyed because of greed that started small and grew big.

Sharper than any two-edged sword? Yes, indeed! And God's word will hurt when it cuts us because it judges the reflections and thoughts of our hearts. Let's continue to store up God's word within us, for as it wounds, so will it heal, if we are willing to change and so share in His holiness.

I Gibbin My Heart to Jesus

How many of you have heard it said that Christmas is for children? As mother of four I can attest to the joy of celebrating this holiday with youngsters around. From the first day of Advent when the Advent wreath comes down and the kids fight over who blows out the candle, until the 24th window is opened on the Advent calendar, anticipation builds in young hearts.

My husband and I try to keep Christ in Christmas by teaching our children about the spiritual significance of this holiday. You'd be surprised how readily little ones seem to respond to the story of our Savior's birth. Every year we decorate a birthday cake for Jesus on Christmas day. Young children have no trouble focusing on the real meaning of Christmas if we do ourselves. Memories of Christmases past now flood my mind.

I recall as a new mother how eager I was to celebrate our baby's first Christmas. With typical new parent enthusiasm, we were so intent on celebrating Jesus' birth that we never took the time to tell Mark about Santa Claus. One December when he was still very young, Mark finally popped the inevitable question. "Who's the fat guy in the red suit?" We had some explaining to do!

Our second son also responded to our presentation of the Christmas story. He knew we'd be thrilled with his Christmas pageant at nursery school. I'll never forget how we had to stifle our laughter as four-year-old Peter proudly announced that he'd been chosen for a part in the nativity play. "I'm one of the three wise guys who look for Jesus!" May he always be such a wise guy.

But more to the point was my daughter Marie-Thérèse who, at the age of three, spent the month of December telling everyone about her Christmas wish. When asked what she wanted for Christmas, Marie-Thérèse would reply, "I gibbin my heart to Jesus." The check-out lady at the grocery store looked puzzled until I explained that my little girl wanted to give Jesus a birthday present for Christmas—the gift of her heart.

Last Christmas I took Patrick, then two, to visit Santa in two malls close to our home. Patrick does know who the "fat guy in the red suit is." By child number four you do these things. After telling Santa that he wanted a football, baseball, and basketball Patrick added, "You know, it's Jesus' birthday!" The first Santa looked dumbfounded. "What?" he asked. Patrick repeated the Good News even louder, "It's Jesus' birthday!" The Santa at the second mall beamed when he heard my child's announcement. "Yes, Patrick," Santa said, "You're right! It is Jesus' birthday. You must love him. I love Him too." Now that's a Santa with the true spirit of St. Nicholas!

Yes, Christmas is the birthday of Jesus and we need to proclaim the "good news of a great joy which shall come to all the people" (Luke 2:10). And, it is this: "God so loved the world that He gave His only Son, that whoever believes in Him should not perish but have eternal life" (John 3:16).

I don't know about you, but I feel challenged by the simple, wholehearted response to the Lord I see in children. I pray that you and I may have the boldness of my son Patrick who wasn't afraid to announce the Good News to Santa Claus himself.

Let's look for opportunities to speak about Jesus and His love in cards, at holiday parties, and family gatherings. Try out a "God bless you" to the clerk in the shopping center. I pray that you and I may delight the Lord by offering Him the same birthday gift as my little one who said, "I gibbin my heart to Jesus." As it says in Isaiah, "A little child shall lead them."

Sister to All

Everyone was scared. It was hard not to whisper while waiting in line, even though Sister had told us to be quiet and pray. My nervousness was steadily increasing as the line was steadily decreasing. Soon it would be my turn to make my first Confession. Would I remember all my sins? What would Father say?

A solemn looking nun sat right next to the entrance of the confessional watching us children as we waited. But her serious expression changed to a giggle when my turn came. She spotted the "thumbs up" sign my girlfriend gave me as she emerged from the confessional. Her "ok" signal put me at ease. Everything really would be all right in there. Sister's laughter helped a lot too.

First Communion preparations constitute my earliest recollections of religious sisters. Sr. Emilina taught my Communion class and even now I can remember the wonderful feeling I had when she would speak about the Lord. She obviously loved God very much because that love emanated from her as she told us Bible stories. The months I spent under her instruction gave me some of my first experiences of the presence of God. Through her I came to know that deep quiet within which is at one and the same time a peace and a longing. Many years later when I was baptized in the Holy Spirit I remembered those early stirrings of hunger for God which dear Sr. Emilina first awakened in me.

Here was a woman who had chosen to consecrate herself totally to God so that she could be a sister to all. Her teaching and her example had a profound effect on my life even though I knew her just a short time. We've all known sisters like Sr. Emilina who have taught, helped, guided and prayed for us over the years. What a tremendous debt of gratitude we in the Church owe to these women who have left all to follow Jesus!

My appreciation for religious sisters grew even more when I received a beautiful letter in the mail recently. It came from a 78-year-old missionary sister in Malaysia. Although we've never met, she reads my columns in *New Covenant* magazine and wrote to me in care of the magazine. Her words were like a bouquet of encouragement and a fountain of prayer that refreshed me. Because I believe that what she wrote can be a source of encouragement to many other lay people who will read this, I'd like to share an excerpt of her letter. Here is a message from a woman who has chosen to be a sister to all of us. She writes,

> *More and more I come to appreciate what you "people in the world" are doing for Christ, totally committed to Him, to His cause, to the Church while taking care of a home, a spouse and growing children! Only a person in your shoes can understand what it all means! I think that when I go to heaven through the mercy of God, I shall have to wonder at the marvels the Lord has done for the brave lay men and women in this 20th Century, who through the great problems and difficulties of the time have reached sanctity.*

> *Courage; you are on the right track. Keep your hands firmly clasped to His, and go confidently ahead in the power of the Spirit joyfully singing as you go along, for the Lord loves you dearly. This is certain!*

What a morale booster!

There are of course, women like Blessed Mother Teresa, and Sr. Briege whose marvelous work is widely known. How reassuring to know that there are also countless other religious sisters we don't read about in the news who are generously serving the people of God in their own special way. In the midst of so much confusion in the Church concerning the role of women religious, there are sisters like these who experience joy and freedom in their vocations.

To this dear sister from Malaysia and the many like her who have helped us follow Jesus, let us offer our support and thanks. The Church needs women such as these. We need women such as these. May they hold fast to their vocations to love Jesus with undivided hearts and continue to serve His people with great dedication. Jesus Himself assures them with these words, "You who have left everything to follow Me; you will have it all returned a hundredfold and will inherit eternal life" (cf. Mark 10:28-30). Thank you, women religious, for being sisters to us all!

 **Breastfeeding**

"Patti, I want you to talk about breastfeeding," the Lord seemed to say.

My heart sank! "Oh, no. I can't, Lord—not here, not now," I protested.

This exchange took place while I was serving as one of the only women team members at a conference entitled *"Totus Tuus"* concerning consecration to Jesus through Mary. One of my functions was to listen to all the presentations and give a final talk to summarize the message of the weekend. Talk about breastfeeding?!! In front of all these priests? How in the world could I relate something as natural as breastfeeding to something as supernatural as consecration to Jesus through Mary?

Deep down I knew I had to obey the prompting of the Holy Spirit, but I needed the assurance that I was really hearing His voice. In His mercy, the Lord provided me with that assurance. Here's how it happened.

On Saturday of the conference, I pulled out my little copy of *The Secret of Mary*, an excerpt of *True Devotion to Mary* by St. Louis de Montfort, a great follower of Jesus and lover of Mary. His act of consecration to Mary is the motto chosen by Pope Saint John Paul II: *Totus Tuus, Maria*—I am all yours, Mary.

To my surprise, as I turned my little book about Mary over, I found on the back cover several notes with phrases like, "baby too sleepy," "temperament" and "bowel movements." Would you believe that these were notes from a conversation with my pediatrician nine years before concerning—you guessed it—breastfeeding of all things! My infant daughter was not nursing well at the time and I had called the doctor for advice.

How amazing God's providence is! Years before He allowed me to record these notes about breastfeeding on a book concerning consecration to Mary. Never would I have imagined there was any connection. Even then He was preparing me to understand and communicate a lesson about His desire for us to come to Mary. Having received so convincing a sign, I felt the courage to share my story. Perhaps it will help you too.

I've had two kinds of babies—those who love to nurse and those who don't. The infants who were eager to breastfeed brought joy to my mother's heart, since everything within me longed to nourish the new life I had brought to birth. The babies who were too sleepy or lazy or reluctant to breastfeed worried me. You see, a mother's milk is perfectly suited to her child's needs. Unlike formula, breast milk is easily digested, produces no excess fat, and will not stain. Breastfed babies do not normally develop allergies as bottle-fed babies do. And as extra protection, a mother's immunities are even passed on to her infant through breast milk!

Besides all the nutritional value of breastfeeding, there is the bonding that occurs when a mother nourishes her child at the breast. What nursing mother has not thrilled to the look of love in her infant's eyes as he explores her face with a tiny hand, while pausing to smile in the midst of a feeding? The nourishment and the mother are inseparable—an intimacy results.

Knowing that my milk would produce such wonderful results, I wept over my babies who would not breastfeed. The only way a mother's milk can enter her child is if the child *takes* it. As much as I tried to interest my reluctant babies, it was ultimately each child's choice to eat or not to eat.

From the cross, Jesus entrusted us to Mary with with His words, "Woman, behold your son." St. John, the beloved disciple, represented all of us. And Jesus entrusted Mary to us, who are all His beloved disciples, in these words, "Son, behold your mother." Mary's role in our lives is to help us grow into the image of Jesus her Son. There are lessons concerning humility, surrender, faith, obedience, purity, courage and perseverance that Mary longs to teach us. She can instruct us better than anyone else in the school of holiness, having formed Jesus first in her womb and then in her home.

Like mother's milk, Mary's teaching is perfectly suited for our growth in Christ. Nothing artificial or harmful ever comes to us through her care. I like to think of receiving her "immunities" as the protection we have against the work of Satan. In Genesis 3:15 we read about the enmity between the woman and the serpent and in Revelations Chapter 12 we see the woman and her offspring triumphing over the attack of the dragon. What child of Mary has not experienced her powerful protection in times of trouble and temptation?

Did you ever wonder why Jesus gave us Mary to be our mother? It's because He knows we need her! Her love and assistance are there for each of us if we would, like St. John, "receive her into our home." Just as I could not force my reluctant infants to take my nourishment, neither does Mary force-feed us. She waits patiently for our response. And how grateful and glad she is when we do respond to her call.

I urge you to consider entrusting yourself to Mary, as your mother. The Father entrusted Jesus to her. Jesus freely submitted himself to her care. The Holy Spirit has been called her Spouse. Countless saints have consecrated themselves to Mary. Pope Saint John Paul II and Blessed Mother Teresa urge consecration to her Immaculate Heart. Can we choose anything better?

From Death to Life

It was 10:30 p.m. at Highland Park Hospital in Covington, Louisiana. Dr. Bill Mitchell, family physician, was about to leave for home when suddenly a woman went into cardiac arrest. The emergency room physician who was treating her needed assistance. As Dr. Mitchell approached the room he began to pray, "Lord, what do You want me to do?" Over and over again he repeated the Lord's name, "Jesus, Jesus, Jesus."

That night the Lord asked Dr. Mitchell to do something which robbed death of a victory. Years ago Bill would have never thought to turn to Jesus in the midst of such a crisis. But things have changed radically for Bill after his conversion and Baptism in the Holy Spirit when he passed from spiritual death to life.

Although Bill was baptized as an infant, he was not raised as a Catholic. After his parents were divorced he lived eight years in a foster home where he received no religious instruction. Bill wasn't aware of what he was missing spiritually because life was very busy with sports and studies. After medical school and internship Bill began his practice. He says he knew about Jesus without really knowing Him personally. Only at Christmas and Easter would he attend Mass.

This was the extent of his spiritual life until Bill's twin brother, Phil, became a believing Christian and began witnessing to him. On January 1, 1982, about midnight while Phil was praying, the Lord spoke to him. "Call Bill now."

At that moment Bill was home alone, feeling depressed. His wife was with her mother who had just been told of a recurrence of cancer. The whole family was upset. Bill wanted desperately to help. If only he could pray for her healing—but he didn't know how.

That night, during an unforgettable phone call, Phil led his brother in a prayer of repentance and commitment to Jesus Christ as his Lord and Savior. As Bill prayed he felt a warmth flow from his head through his entire body. He knew that God was touching him. But Bill still had some doubts about praying with his mother-in-law for healing.

He felt he needed more faith. Just weeks before, Phil and his wife had been baptized in the Holy Spirit. "Let's ask God to baptize you in the Holy Spirit, Bill. That will give you more faith and confidence," said Phil. Bill held the phone in his hand and leaned forward intently. As he asked to receive the Baptism in the Holy Spirit, the power of God rushed on him with such force that he was knocked back in his chair where he remained for 15 minutes. Deliverance and healing took place during that time.

When he rose to his feet, Dr. Bill Mitchell knew that he was a different man. God had raised him from death to life spiritually. The heaviness Bill had carried around for years was gone. In its place was peace, joy and a tremendous faith in God's healing love. Bill has witnessed many healings since then, including the one in the emergency room.

The woman on the emergency room bed had no productive heartbeat. She had been electroshocked in an attempt to reestablish a heartbeat, but it had failed. She was not breathing. The emergency room physician was doing external cardiac massage and the nurses were ventilating her. Bill came and stood at the foot of her bed. The Lord spoke to him. "Bind Satan in My name, and in My name loose her." Things were moving fast.

This was a tough order with two nurses and a doctor standing by, but Bill was obedient. He laid hands on her and repeated the word of command God had given him. At that instant her heart started beating loud and clear on the monitor. Beep. Beep. Beep. What a welcome sound!

Once again the Lord spoke to Bill. "Cast the spirit of death out of her, and My spirit of life into her in My name, the name of Jesus." Bill obeyed. Immediately the woman sat up, vomited and looked at Bill.

"How do you feel?" he asked.

"I feel fine," she answered.

And she was. She recovered completely from her heart attack and was soon released. God had intervened on her behalf and snatched her from the jaws of death through the obedience of His servant.

As glorious as it is to see a physical life restored, more glorious still is the transformation from death to life spiritually. Ask Dr. Bill Mitchell. He knows.

Show Me that You Are My Mother

I just had a delightful time sharing with some folks who went on a Marian pilgrimage with me in June, 1990. By the end of our trip we felt like brothers and sisters, and it's no wonder. We discover we are indeed members of the same family. And isn't that one of the marvelous charisms of a mother—to bring her children together?

When we think of Marian devotion, we immediately think of the Rosary. We're asked to pray the rosary daily for peace. It is a prayer Mary loves. However, if you are one who has difficulty with this form of prayer, take heart! Please don't conclude you are outside your heavenly mother's love. She accepts you just as you are, and wants you to approach her in whatever way you can at this time. You see, I'm a mother and I know. Perhaps the following story will illustrate my point.

My two older sons are equally precious to me, yet each boy used to approach me differently when they were young. One of them would say, "Mom, I can see you're busy now, but when you can schedule it, I'd like to talk to you." Can you believe it? At that stage in his life he was usually full of consideration, respect, and gratitude.

My other son loves me just as much, however, his approach to me as a child was significantly more casual. One day I called home and our conversation ran something like this:

"Hi, Son. This is Mom."

"Yo Dude!" he responded.

("Yo Dude!", I think. I'm his mother!) "How's everything, Son?"

"No problem. Hey, Ma, you know that picture of the Holy Father in the den? Well, I really needed a picture frame, so I figured you wouldn't mind if I took the Holy Father's picture out and put mine in. Now, don't say anything yet, 'til you see how good my school play photo looks in your frame. I mean, Ma, you got so many holy pictures around the house already. Hey, Ma, I love ya."

"I know you do, Son. I love you too."

Both are my boys. Both love me. Both are precious to me. Both need me. And I'm convinced that God has a wonderful plan for both of their lives. As a mother I want to do all I can to help each child discover and fulfill God's will. I'm no less eager to form and guide the son who "stole" my picture frame!

My one son might represent that person who lovingly prays the rosary daily, and wears a scapular, medal, or some outward sign of his consecration to Mary. The other son might represent someone equally in need of his heavenly mother's love and assistance, but not quite ready for formal expressions of love and devotion. His exchanges with Mary might be in the form of spontaneous cries for help along the journey to God. This child may not even realize how much his mother is obtaining for him by her prayer, but he is receiving it nonetheless.

The point is this: *Turn to Mary now in whatever way you can.* She loves the rosary and asks you to pray it. But if you are not presently faithful to the daily rosary, don't close your heart to a relationship with Our Lady. Her mother's heart is infinitely big enough to understand and welcome you just as you are. Speak to her in your own words. Open your heart to her in simplicity as a child. She loves you. She wants to help you. Even baby steps in her direction please her.

I've recently discovered an ancient prayer of St. Simon Stock to Our Lady of Mt. Carmel that contains a phrase I'd love to place on everyone's lips. The phrase is this: *"Show me that you are my mother."* Just ask her to show you that she is your mother. And she will.

The Angel of the Lord

I recently returned from taping some shows at EWTN located on the grounds of Our Lady of the Angels Monastery. As I admired the many depictions of angels on the monastery grounds, my thoughts turned to several experiences of the past year concerning guardian angels.

In the past I'd say an occasional prayer for the assistance of angels, but I never got very specific, nor did I pray directly to guardian angels. One day, Al and I had to be out of town for the weekend and I was feeling apprehensive about leaving our four children. I knew our trip was in God's will, but I still felt uneasy. Then it occurred to me to pray to each child's guardian angel for protection and for a pleasant weekend. My mind was suddenly at peace and I was able to enter my weekend responsibilities worry-free.

Upon our return I was amazed to discover that each child had some positive spiritual experience during that time. For instance, one of my children picked up the book *Miracles of the Eucharist* and was fascinated by it. If we had asked him to read it, he would have probably refused. Another child took part in a rosary group with some friends. Could it be, I wondered, that my specific prayer to each child's guardian angel had some effect?

Then recently I was leading our annual Holy Spirit Women's Retreat for 200 women. A few days before the retreat, I began to feel apprehensive. So many women. So many needs. So many potential problems. Some were coming from great distances. I anticipated that our team might be too small to provide all the support needed. Then it dawned on me that I should quit worrying and start praying.

Spontaneously this was the prayer that arose out of my heart, "Lord, if I'll have less human support, I expect more heavenly support for this retreat. I pray to the guardian angels of the women coming. Protect their travels. Minister good thoughts to them. Help them respond to God. Let them have a great desire to surrender their lives to Him."

I've never prayed that way before, but I can tell you this. I'll do it every time I minister in the future! From the first session these 200 women were ready for God—open, eager, hungry. Usually it takes a while for people to relax and let go of their burdens enough to enter into a retreat fully. Not this time! Almost fifty women were baptized in the Holy Spirit in an explosion of joy and praise. The gift of tongues was released with power. Repentance poured forth. People were healed. Sr. Linda Koontz, who travels extensively, was with us and remarked how extraordinary the retreat was. Peace prevailed in personal relationships. Team members were free of the usual hassles we expect in the midst of a spiritual undertaking.

By the way, no one knew about my prayer to the guardian angels. But after the retreat, I received the following reports from women whom I know to be spiritually mature. One said that as I opened the retreat Friday night she saw a large angel standing next to me. Another said that at the prayer meeting she heard angelic voices praising God above us. Several others said they heard the swishing sound of angel wings passing in our midst during the weekend. Coincidental? Imaginary? Childlike? I think not.

Since then, I've learned that when Pope Saint John XXIII anticipated a difficult meeting, he would pray to his guardian angel and the guardian angel of the person with whom he would be speaking. There was a noticeable peace which resulted.

Let's ask the Holy Spirit what He wants to teach us about guardian angels for our own protection, the welfare of our loved ones and the effectiveness of our ministry. Maybe it's time to rediscover the prayer of our youth.

Angel of God, my guardian dear,
to whom God's love entrusts me here,
ever this day be at my side
to light and guard, to rule and guide.
Amen.

For All You Do

November and December are busy months for most people, but in my family they are especially so. In addition to Thanksgiving and Christmas, we have birthdays and anniversaries of many of our relatives. Like most women, I'm the one who is responsible for planning celebrations, making or purchasing gifts, sending cards, and trying to make these occasions festive. Although I try to start my preparations early, by the end of the holiday season I'm usually exhausted.

Because I was getting worn out, my husband insisted one day last holiday season that I go back to bed after the children left for school. I didn't need much convincing, so I tucked myself in. When I opened my eyes, on the pillow beside me was a long-stemmed red rose with a note attached which read, "For all you do, this bud's for you."

For once those familiar words from the Budweiser beer commercial were a delight to me! My husband knew I needed more than just rest to carry me through this demanding time. I needed some words of appreciation and support to encourage me in serving my family during the holidays.

Mothers need to be appreciated. (Hear, hear!!) But then, so do fathers, children, grandparents, priests, sisters and brothers. We who are following the Lord want to serve Him willingly and joyfully in all circumstances. How we wish we could do this day in and day out, year in and year out, without a word of appreciation or thanks. But most of us will readily admit that expressions of gratitude, especially from those close to us, make a real difference. When someone seems so secure that he or she doesn't need to receive praise or recognition, don't be fooled. "Just because water rolls off a duck's back, doesn't mean the duck doesn't like it."

Sometimes before we hear words of gratitude from others, we have to learn to speak them. We can spend out time bemoaning the fact that no one ever thanks us when we've rarely uttered a word of thanks ourselves. Try starting with simple things like: "Thanks for taking out the garbage." "Thanks for helping with the yard." "I appreciate your good report card." "This is a great meal."

I read about a woman who chose Thanksgiving Day to tell her husband of forty years how much she appreciated him. She let him know how secure she felt in his love. She complimented him for the way he had provided for their family and protected them; even in bad times he was always there. More than the Thanksgiving feast she prepared that day, her words had nourished her husband. He strutted around for the rest of that day like a peacock because she took the time to express her gratitude.

There may be expensive gifts we cannot afford to purchase for our loved ones. Yet through our words we have a wonderful way to enrich their lives. Scripture says, "Like dew that abates a burning wind, so does a word improve a gift. *Sometimes the word means more than the gift...*" (Sirach 18:15-16).

We can celebrate Thanksgiving all year long by expressing our genuine appreciation to those closest to us for all they are and for all they do.

P. S. For any men who may have read this: Long-stemmed roses may be purchased for just a few dollars. What an investment in your future!

9 Wholeheartedness

Is it possible there is another woman out there who has either married or given birth to a football fan? Somehow I didn't find out about my husband's love for football until after we were married. Slowly but surely I realized that when he said he just wanted to "catch the score" it involved much more than a few minues in front of the television set!

When our first son, Mark, came along one of his first toys was—you guessed it—a tiny football. He eagerly looked forward to his dad's arrival home from work every day, greeting him with the words "Hup, hup! Play pootball, Dada?" As he grew, so did his interest in the sport. Al taught him everything he knew about the game. I'll never forget my amazement to hear this little child speak authoritatively about the plays used in a game that took place before he was even born!

When our second son, Peter, arrived it was only natural that he should take a lively interest in football as well. Learning his colors wasn't a mere matter of red or blue, but red for the Georgia Bulldogs and blue for Notre Dame's Fighting Irish. Then came the endless football jerseys, jackets, caps and school bags with football insignias. There were the football garbage cans, sheets, curtains, lamps and bedspreads. In answer to the question, "What do you want for your birthday?", I usually hear about football pennants, football magazines, football calendars, pencils, cups and posters. Did you know there are even football pushpins to attach football clippings to your football bulletin board?!

A few years ago the boys discovered football cards—the kind you trade. These cards are like silver and gold to my sons. Why they are interested in all the statistics about each player, I'll never know. But they are.

You women who have fans in your home realize that every game is important to a true fan. When I propose some activity that may conflict with a particular game, my son, Mark, waxes eloquent on how crucial this very game is to the entire season!

I thought I knew the extent of my sons' interest in football until just recently when the family spent several hours in the car on a trip. The boys were speaking excitedly to one another in high pitched voices about something I couldn't decipher. Then my husband explained to me that they were playing sportscasters for an imaginary football game. One was doing the "play by play" and the other was doing the "color!" This kept them busy for hours.

These two young boys with their tremendous, all-consuming love for every aspect of football have shown me something about what wholeheartedness means. Even though I don't share my boys' enthusiasm for football, I've always admired the virtue of wholeheartedness.

As a young girl I remember reading about Anna Pavlova, the famous ballerina, whose whole life was given up for the dance. The beauty of ballet had captivated her. For Pavlova "to live was to dance." Later I was deeply impressed by the dedication of a forest ranger whose love for nature consumed him. The beauty of the outdoors had captivated him. Eventually I discovered the lives of the saints whose passion was neither for the dance nor the forest, but for God Himself. The beauty of the Lord of all had captivated their hearts. He was first in their thoughts, in their conversations and in their activities. Falling in love with God had transformed every aspect of their lives.

You and I are called to be saints as well, people who are wholeheartedly for the Lord. We are to be His fans, His friends, His promoters. We are to surround ourselves with reminders of Him, study all we can about Him, immerse ourselves in all that concerns Him, talk about Him, sing to Him, serve Him, love Him.

To those who do not understand, it may seem like we've given over too much of our time, our thoughts, our resources and our lives to Him. Yet who is more worthy of such devotion than our God? And the example of a wholehearted believer has tremendous power to draw others to faith. As they see our dedication may they come to know and love this glorious Lord Jesus Christ whom we serve.

Scripture tells us, "The eyes of the Lord roam over the whole earth to encourage those who are devoted to Him *wholeheartedly*" (II Chronicles 16:9). As His eyes roam over the earth today, may He be pleased to find in you and me a wholehearted devotion to the glory of His name. Amen.

Thanks, But No Thanks

Dear Grandma,

Thanks so much for the birthday gift.
You always manage to pick out something I really like.

I love you.

Peter

I happened to see this note of thanks after our son's last birthday. We try to teach our children the importance of thanking others for their generosity, gifts and time. Haven't we all had the experience of sending a gift and never receiving an acknowledgement? That hurts. We feel we have a right to expect a word of thanks, and we do. In the realm of human relationships, columnist Miss Manners would agree. It's impolite to receive a gift without thanking the donor.

We should graciously accept thanks when it's given, but we have to also learn not to expect thanks, depending on the circumstances. It may be customary to receive thanks for a gift you've given a friend. But if you carry that same expectation into your Christian ministry, it can hinder your service.

As Christians we're called to be like Jesus who came to serve, not to be served. We're to look to other's interests rather than our own. Jesus' service emanated from His love and obedience to the Father and His love for us. He is our model in ministry. If we're serving out of a desire to be noticed, appreciated, or needed, we will become quickly discouraged. Our service must be rendered "as to the Lord," out of gratitude for all He has done for us. Any thanks we receive from others is, as we say in New Orleans, "lagniappe." That means "extra," like the thirteenth donut of a baker's dozen.

This lesson came home to me on retreat. During prayer I found myself remembering a situation in ministry when I felt misunderstood and unappreciated. "Nobody even realized how much I sacrificed," I mused.

Then I sensed the Lord speak to me interiorly, "Thank you for being there for Me." Against the backdrop of His word of thanks, all I could see was my own self-centeredness. "But, Lord, I wasn't there completely for Your sake. In part I guess I was looking for recognition and esteem from others."

Have you ever experienced a situation like this? It's one of those "But, Lord..." conversations where you know He's about to light up a truth for you and there's no escape. I felt like St. Peter protesting, "No, Lord, you will never wash my feet." The Lord Himself was thanking me. He repeated it interiorly in my heart, "Thank you for being there for Me."

How could I accept thanks from God after seeing how selfish my service actually was? But do you know, I could not leave that prayer time in chapel without accepting His thanks. "You're welcome, Lord," I muttered sheepishly.

"Now when you remember that situation in the future," He seemed to say, "don't ever complain to Me that you weren't thanked. I Myself thanked you."

Gulp! In one brief encounter with the Lord I learned I must be content to minister for Him alone and to receive thanks from Him alone. Of course, we still often experience appreciation from others. But that cannot be sustenance to us, just lagniappe. "Whatever your task, work heartily, as serving the Lord and not men, knowing that from the Lord you will receive the inheritance as your reward; you are serving the Lord Christ" (Colossians 3:23-24).

How many Christians in ministry have become discouraged and burned out because they expected to be loved and appreciated for their service? Thanksgiving Day did not occur every time they washed someone's feet. What a rude awakening! Those we serve haven't necessarily read Miss Manners. They may not even want to receive the gift we're giving.

Someone commented to me recently about my travels, "You must enjoy going about the country and speaking at conferences." Yes, but there's a great danger in it too. In a conference setting it's common to receive praise for your ministry. That's not everyday reality for a servant of the Lord. The true measure of our Christian service comes as we work faithfully and lovingly in hidden ways even when no one says thanks.

As I was preparing these reflections, a prayer card arrived in the mail with a picture of Pope Saint John Paul II. On the other side of the card in the Holy Father's own handwriting, was a quote from Romans 12:11, *"He whom you serve is the Lord."* The Lord and Master of the house sees well what His servants are doing for Him. Let's joyfully thank Him for the privilege of being His servants and humbly receive His thanks in return.

Members of the Family

Shortly after I was baptized in the Spirit I paid a visit to some of my Dad's relatives. Living with them was an elderly Irish woman we called Aunt Maggie. Although she was not related to us by blood, I always thought of her as a member of the family. I didn't know Aunt Maggie well, but on this occasion I was impressed by the fact that she was praying the rosary when I arrived. After our visit I asked her to pray for me when she said her rosary. Being new in my walk with the Lord, I wanted to benefit from her prayers.

Aunt Maggie grabbed my hand and gazed intently into my eyes. "Oh, I will, I will," she said. "I'll pray for you now, but even more so later." Then she smiled and kissed me. By "later" I knew she meant that after her death she would continue to pray for me and those she loved. I never saw Aunt Maggie again but I trust that when she went home to be with the Lord, she remembered her promise to me.

"I'll pray for you now, but even more so later." Aunt Maggie's words capture so well the reality of the relationship we have with Christians who have gone before us. We can pray for those who are still in need of our help. And we can benefit from the intercession of those who are already in heaven.

Within the Church we honor men and women officially called saints. They are our brothers and sisters in Christ who have "fought the good fight, finished the race, kept the faith, and merited the crown" (II Timothy 4:7). Spiritually, we really are members of the same family because of what Jesus has done for us all. Have you ever experienced the joy and power of having one of the saints as a special friend? I have.

From the time I was just a little girl I loved St. Thérèse of Lisieux. Before I knew anything about her life, I chose her as my friend just because she was depicted with a bouquet of roses. Since I loved roses and my nickname was Rosebud, I assumed Thérèse and I had something in common.

Later as I read her autobiography, I came to love her tremendous humility, her faith, her confidence in God's mercy and her "Little Way" of doing even the smallest things out of great love for God. The better I got to know St. Thérèse, the easier it was to pray to her in times of need. I chose her as my patroness at Confirmation and when my daughter was born, it was only natural to name my own little flower, Marie-Thérèse At the end of her brief life St. Thérèse said, "I feel that my mission is soon to begin...I will spend my heaven doing good upon earth." To those who entreat her, St. Thérèse promised to send a "shower of roses." Over and over again I've experienced this shower of roses in my life.

For example, there was the time I prayed to St. Thérèse about a situation with one of my sons. Within moments a neighbor unexpectedly brought over some cuttings from her rosebush. The situation worked out in my child's best interests. Another time I asked Thérèse's intercession before speaking at an important conference. As I finished the talk there was an aroma of roses. The day I began a novena to St. Thérèse for the health of my unborn child, a woman at our prayer meeting surprised me with a beautiful red rose.

Countless are the testimonies of St. Thérèse's friends on earth who have felt the power of her prayers from heaven. I know of a woman who was longing for a new baby after having had several miscarriages. The very day she began a novena to St. Thérèse for this intention, her husband felt prompted to bring her flowers. Instead of buying daisies, her favorite flowers, he chose a rose. He knew nothing of her novena. Within a year she conceived and now has a beautiful baby girl—Maria Theresa!

Like every saint, Thérèse loved Jesus with her whole heart while on earth and delights to make Him known and loved by helping us from heaven. You may not feel you can relate to her, but there is surely some saint whose life and charisms you can admire. Find a saint you can call on as a special friend. It may be the saint whose name you bear or some other saint whose virtues attract you.

There is the humility of St. Francis, the faithfulness of St. Joseph, the simplicity of St. Bernadette, the strength of St. Ignatius, the gentleness of St. Francis de Sales, the boldness of St. Catherine, the zeal of St. Patrick. Get to know the saints. They're ready to show you how to love God more. After all, we're members of the same family!

Carpooling

Ever feel like you're spending most of your life in the car? Take Wednesday for example. 11:45 a.m.: "Baby Carpool," with Patrick and several of his little friends. Conversation? Well, Mickey told me that his mommy has a new baby in her tummy, and Ryan explained three times why he needed a Superman Band Aid on his finger.

Precious cargo delivered, Patrick and I hit the road again. Sherwin-Williams for paint. Cloth World for fabric. Eckerds for prescriptions. Before I knew it, time for my "Big Boy Carpool" had arrived. "Never be late," is one of the cardinal rules my two teenage sons have impressed on me.

As I sat in the parking lot of the high school, waiting for seven teenage boys to pile into the van, I reviewed the other carpool rules my sons have stressed. It must be wearisome for teenagers to have to train their parents!

1. Turn off all music! If you like it, the guys won't!

2. Slang from the fifties and sixties is banned. "Cool" and "neat" are out!

3. Current teenage jargon should never pass a mom's lips. "Awesome" and "radical" are forbidden.

4. Don't ask embarrassing questions like, "How is school coming?"

5. Don't call attention to the fact you're even there behind the wheel.

6. Who wants his mom to still drive him when he's in high school anyway?

After car pool, I drove uptown for Mark's doctor appointment, then to shop for a new pair of pants. By the time I brought him home, I needed to pick up my cheerleader. One more jaunt back to the high school to drop Peter at Open House! Tired yet? I saw an ad for a mini van recently that read like this: *Whoever invented the term "Stay-at-home Mom" should have his head examined!*

Of course, not every day is as busy as Wednesday, but I hope this description has convinced you that I'm living in the real world like you, finding very little quiet or contemplation built into a typical day. Yet, there are ways to live in the presence of God on even the most hectic carpool days.

For instance, when alone in the car, I play Christian tapes— sometimes a teaching, the rosary, or music. You'd be amazed how the Lord can minister to you as you sing His praises even in the midst of a traffic jam! Then there are times I just pray in tongues, interceding according to the mind of God. "We know not how to pray but the Spirit helps us in our weakness" (cf. Romans 8:26).

As I pass certain places, I extend my hand in prayer and blessing. For example, once my car broke down, and a kind woman let me use her phone. Now every time I pass her home I call down the Lord's blessing on her. My husband and I pray daily against the activities in an abortion clinic on our route. If I pass a Catholic church, I make the sign of the cross or bow my head to acknowledge the real presence of Jesus in the tabernacle.

When I'm in the car with only one of my kids, I use those few moments to give that child some individual attention through a question, compliment or correction. In my "Baby Carpool", I'm not bound by the teenage rules, so I can freely share Jesus with these little ones. Sometimes I play a Bible song tape, and the van rocks to a chorus of "This Little Light of Mine, I'm Gonna Let It Shine." Yes, I even prayed for Ryan's finger right there in the van, and I assured Mickey that he's going to be a good big brother to that new little baby in his mommy's tummy.

With my "Big Boy Carpool" I'm more discreet. But you'd better believe that I'm talking to Jesus silently about the needs I see in the young men I cart back and forth. Like the short kid who's surrounded by tall guys like my Mark, or the fellow who lost a brother to suicide, or the one who never has his papers together neatly or...Well, you get the point.

Carpooling can be a time-consuming task. It's easy to grumble about it. But there is another alternative. We parents can seize every moment, even those in the car, to draw closer to God and to make Him known to the children in our care. Safe, happy and Spirit-filled driving to you all!

The Ski Sweater

Many of you who have read my columns over the years tell me that you feel as though you know my family. And you do. In fact, I consider you part of my extended family all over the world. I had been planning to tell you a story involving my dad this month, but the story is all the more meaningful to me now since I have just returned from the funeral of my beloved father, Peter A. Gallagher.

What a privilege to be at Daddy's side during his final days. As I held his hand, I reminded him that it's because of the love that he's lavished on me, that I can have such confidence in my heavenly Father. Daddy was a beautiful mirror of a generous, loving God. Outstanding qualities? Well, nothing flashy. Self-educated. Hardworking. Kind. Affectionate. Thoughtful. His dry wit and marvelous Irish tenor voice filled our home with laughter and music. And he was there for us. Always there.

Daddy was one of those unusual men who actually loved to shop. This meant that Mother and the four of us kids would receive gifts that Daddy had selected himself. I can still see him toting in a rocking horse for my little brother, Peter, days before Christmas. Then there were the roses he brought me when I had strep throat at age four! My delight in the bouquet moved him to promise me a rose on every birthday. In fact, just a few days before he was admitted to the intensive care unit, Pete Gallagher picked out yet *another* bottle of perfume for his sweetheart of 47 years, Netta. No special occasion. Just a token of love.

My story is about one of Daddy's gifts to me on Christmas, well over 20 years ago. Under the tree, I spied a package marked, "To Patti—Love, Daddy." I opened it eagerly, knowing how beautiful his gifts always were. Hopefully my face did not betray the disappointment in my heart. While I usually liked Daddy's selections, this time his choice was not at all to my taste.

He had bought me a brightly colored ski sweater with a striped pattern that went horizontally—not the way most short girls want their stripes to go! I thanked him, of course, and I didn't dare exchange it for fear of hurting his feelings. As I returned to my job in another state, I was quite certain that I would never wear that unbecoming ski sweater.

But in the months that followed, I found that the ski sweater began to appeal to me after all, especially because my own father had selected it. Not many girls had dads who shopped for them. My dad had. In time, that ski sweater became a precious symbol of my father's love for me, my father's choice concerning me, my father's pleasure in gifting me. I began to wear it with pride—not simply in the gift, but in the love of the giver.

Here's the amazing thing! Over 20 years later, I still have that sweater! Of all the clothes I have purchased for myself, not one article of clothing has remained in my wardrobe as long as this ski sweater has. I just can't part with it. In fact, I even wore it during one of my last visits with Daddy in the hospital before he died.

Through this simple incident the Spirit has taught me a lesson. Sometimes our Father in heaven chooses something for us that is not to our immediate liking. But if He is the one who has chosen it, then it bears the mark of His love. As we accept His choice, His will, and "put it on," so to speak, we begin to find that there is pleasure in receiving whatever is offered by

His loving hand. "In His will is our peace." It is always for our good—always a gift. At least, that's what Daddy's ski sweater has taught me.

As we honor our earthly fathers, both living and dead, let's pledge ourselves to honor our heavenly Father by accepting whatever He has chosen for us in His love.

In Memoriam
Peter A. Gallagher
December 6, 1910 – January 23, 1992

Married for the Lord

When I was a little girl I asked my mom countless times, "Please tell me again how you and Daddy met." I'm sure I was not the only child who never tired of hearing the story of my parents' first meeting and courtship. Such stories delight me still. On a recent trip home to New Jersey I had lunch with my parents' friends, Mary and Lou Rose. We were reminiscing over old times and the romantic in me asked, "How did you two meet?"

Lou then recounted how he was sipping a chocolate soda one day in Kless' diner in Irvington, New Jersey, when he spotted Mary with her pony tail and bobby sox. Immediately he was attracted and asked a mutual friend to introduce them. On their first date, Lou, who is now a florist, arrived at Mary's home with a bouquet of flowers. The flowers were not for Mary, but for her mother. What a smart man! That night Lou decided he would marry Mary in six months, and he did! Now almost 50 years later, they're still in love. (Sigh!) After hearing Mary and Lou's romantic story, I decided to share my own, especially since they didn't realize they had a part it.

As I was growing up I always pictured myself married and with a family someday. Yet lurking in the back of my mind was the fear that if I got too close to God, He might want me to be a nun. After surrendering my life to Him in the Baptism in the Holy Spirit, I prayed earnestly to know God's will concerning my vocation. Some friends who had chosen a celibate life told me they wanted to be "single for the Lord." Being totally dedicated to the Lord appealed to me greatly, and so did marriage. Viewing marriage simply in terms of "self-fulfillment" misses the dimension of marriage as a vocation to serve God. I determined I wanted to give my life totally to God as a married person, to become holy as a wife and mother. The way I expressed my deepest desire was that I wanted to be, not "single for the Lord", but "married for the Lord." The "for the Lord" part was crucial to me.

I began to pray that the Lord would bring into my life a man who loved Him above all else, a man dedicated to building God's Kingdom, a man with a vocation to be my husband. For many years I wondered how God could fulfill this desire. Then I discovered a wonderful promise in Psalm 37:4: "Take delight in the Lord and He will give you the desires of your heart." The Lord was telling me that in whatever state I found myself, I should make Him my only joy, and He would grant my heart's requests. I then realized that I could be content spending my time in ministry to the needs of others, trusting the Lord to meet my own need.

"In due time I will act with speed" (Isaiah 60:22). This passage took on new meaning for me in the spring of 1973 as I realized what was happening in my relationship with Al Mansfield. For many years we had been good friends and co-workers. Gradually I came to realize that our friendship was growing into a deeper love.

One Saturday in May, Al invited me out. That whole day was so special starting when the doorbell rang early in the morning. To my surprise my florist friends, Mary and Lou Rose from New Jersey, had wired me a dozen red roses. It was their way of thanking me for a card I had sent them. When the roses arrived I immediately thought of my patroness, St. Thérèse of Lisieux, who promised to send from heaven a shower of roses upon those who requested her intercession. "You'd almost think I had been making a novena to St. Thérèse," I said to myself.

There was a chapel in the home in which I lived at the time, so I placed the roses in front of the Blessed Sacrament, my favorite prayer spot. This was the last day our household would enjoy the privilege of having the Blessed Sacrament in our chapel. A Mass was celebrated that afternoon and all the hosts were consumed.

As Al and I walked along the shore of Lake Pontchartrain later that night, he told me he was in love with me. From that moment on, my life has never been the same. In him I have found the wisdom, the kindness, strength and manly holiness I was searching for in a husband.

When I returned home after our date I went into the chapel and sat before the empty tabernacle. Though His Real Presence in the Blessed Sacrament was absent I still heard the Lord speak in the depths of my heart. "Do you see how much I love you? The very day I am no longer present to you in the way you've come to know and love Me here, I am now present to you in a new way through Al." God had answered my prayer.

Imagine my delight the next day to discover that my mother in New Jersey had just completed a novena to St. Thérèse, asking her intercession for the right man to come into my life. That explained my shower of roses!

Marriage is indeed a sacrament—a way to meet Jesus, to love Him and experience His love. What a privilege married couples have in their call to be one that the world may believe in the covenant love of God for His people. December 22nd Al and I will celebrate another anniversary. Each year, with God's grace, we are more in love with each other and more determined to be "married for the Lord," for His glory and the spread of His Kingdom.

His promise has been fulfilled in our lives. May it be fulfilled in yours as well. "Take delight in the Lord, and He will give you the desires of your heart" (Psalm 37:4).

Al and Patti Mansfield on their 40th Anniversary,
December 22, 2013 with
Patrick, Marie-Thérèse, Peter and Mark

The Gospel of December 22 every year
"just happens to be" Mary's Magnificat!

Other Resources by Patti Mansfield

Books:

Magnificat: A Mother's Reflections on Mary

As By A New Pentecost: The Dramatic Beginning of the Catholic Charismatic Renewal

Teaching CDs including:

The Duquesne Weekend: My Personal Testimony

Holiness

More Than Conquerors: Lessons in Spiritual Warfare

Seeking the Face of Jesus

Consecration to Mary

Be Mary

The Gift of Tongues Explained

Women Encounter the Love of Jesus

Come Holy Spirit!

Do You Want to Be Baptized in the Spirit?

Yielding to the Charismatic Gifts

To order these books and teaching CDs, please contact the Author:

Patti Gallagher Mansfield
Catholic Charismatic Renewal of New Orleans
P.O. Box 7515
Metairie, LA 70010-7515

Tel: 504-828-1368
email: info@ccrno.org
www.ccrno.org